A Zebra
in a
Field of Horses

One Parent's Candid Truth About
Raising a Child with Special Needs

Kelly C. Miltimore, BSN, RN

This book is dedicated, first and foremost, to my children, Liam and Mira. You both have taught me more about myself than I could have ever dreamed. I am so incredibly grateful to be your mother!

I would also like to dedicate this book to my parents, Colin and Patricia. There has never been a journey I have set out on that both of you didn't support. The foundation upon which you raised me gave me the confidence to believe I could accomplish anything I set my mind to.

Additionally, I'd like to acknowledge my entire extended family. We have all grown so much during this extraordinary journey. In particular, I'd like to recognize my sister, Shannon, and stepmom, Susanne. Both of you supported me in ways that I will never be able to put into words.

To my amazing friends who stood by me when I no longer had the strength to stand alone, I will be forever grateful for your love and backing. I can't imagine traveling the road less traveled without each and every one of you by my side. Thank you all from the bottom of my heart!

Contents

Introduction   vii

Chapter 1   How Does One Qualify as a Zebra
Rather Than a Horse?   1

Chapter 2   The Beginning of the Beginning   5

Chapter 3   Maybe It's Me? Maybe I Just Suck!   13

Chapter 4   Do I Have Munchausen Syndrome?   17

Chapter 5   What Do Seven Diagnoses Look
Like When You Put Them in a Blender?   23

Chapter 6   Candlelit Dinners While Raising a Child
with Special Needs—
Is That an Oxymoron?   29

Chapter 7   I Am a Boiling Frog   37

Chapter 8   Please Don't Tell Me How to Get
My Baby to Sleep: How Unwanted Advice
Can Make Us Crazy!   41

Chapter 9   When We Know Better, We Do Better   47

Chapter 10   I Wish There Was More I Could
Do to Help!   53

Chapter 11   You Will Get There When You Get
There, and Not a Moment Too Soon!   59

Chapter 12   If You're Lucky, Life Is Humbling!   87

Chapter 13   And Then There Were Two   93

Chapter 14   Thank God for Grandparents! I Think
I'm Going to Choke Them!   99

Chapter 15 Where Are All the Casserole Dishes?   107
Chapter 16 Living in the Moment While Waiting
            for the Other Shoe to Drop   113
Chapter 17 Nothing Ever Turns Out Quite
            How We Imagined   117
Chapter 18 To Med or Not to Med, That Is
            the Question!   123
Chapter 19 Dating When You Live in a Special-
            Needs World   129
Chapter 20 You Really Need to Take Care of Yourself   133
Chapter 21 The Gift Has Yet to Be Revealed   141
Chapter 22 There Is Always Hope!   145
Appendix A The Power of Words   147
Appendix B Motivating Music   151

Introduction

I believe there are gifts in everything and that often the gifts are yet to be revealed. My life has been proof of both, and I take solace in these thoughts when I am at my lowest moments. I have learned to believe a lot of things. I say "learned to believe" because life has a way of teaching us things we never wanted to know.

Much of what I have learned has been from the gift of having a son with special needs. But then there were the gifts of being a mother to a daughter who has a brother with special needs, being a daughter to parents who have a grandchild with special needs, being a wife to a husband who has a son with special needs, being a sister to an aunt who has a nephew with special needs, and being a friend to a person who has a son with special needs. It took me a long time to realize this was happening to all of them too. We were all having our very own experiences, and we each learned so much.

This book is meant to share my journey. I want to share this journey not because I think my story is any more special or interesting than anyone else's, nor because I think I have the answers or even know the right questions to ask, for that matter. I want to share it because I remember feeling so alone for such a long time, and if I can make one person's journey a little less lonely, then I will feel like I've been successful. I have a dear friend, Heather, who has a special little guy too, and when we became friends, she told me she felt as if she'd finally met a fellow zebra in a field of horses. What a gift her friendship has been! I want to be a fellow zebra to those who still feel alone in the field.

I need to warn you in advance: I am *not* going to tell you that landing in this special-needs field is going to be all sunshine and rainbows. I am not going to tell you that you will one day feel at complete peace about where you landed. I am going to tell you that some days you will desperately wish you were a horse and other days you will just want to lie down and never get up again but you will. I am going to tell you how I have learned to laugh at things others find unfathomable because, with gratitude and humility, I have been able to appreciate things most people would find disappointing. I am going to hope that after reading this book you will be proud to be a zebra and wear your stripes standing tall and assured that there's nothing you can't do!

Chapter 1

How Does One Qualify as a Zebra Rather Than a Horse?

I told you in the introduction that I have come to believe a lot of things. One of those things is that people just want to figure out where in the heck they fit! Very early on, in childhood actually, we all try to figure out where we fit. It's like, "OK, I get it; I am a girl. But am I a girly girl or a tomboy? Do I want to be a jock, or do I fit in a bit more with the bookworms?" Then there are the expectations of everyone around you: your mom's telling you how she was a tomboy "just like you," but your aunt keeps buying dresses for you, and your grandma wants you to play tea party. You are pretty sure that none of it feels like a match, but you don't know what feels right either.

For me, this is kind of what it felt like when I was initially trying to navigate the world of being a mother to a child with special needs. It is such a broad term, and for my little guy there wasn't a one-size-fits-all diagnosis. He had some pretty serious sensory issues that were being labeled as sensory processing disorder (SPD), but was that "special" enough? By about age four Liam was autistic-ish, but I just couldn't figure out which day he seemed different enough from all the other kids that I should take him to someone and say, "My kid's kind of odd." What kind of mother thinks that, let alone says it out loud?

I always knew Liam was special, but all of a sudden he qualified as having special needs. By age six, it was official—he had Asperger's syndrome. By age eight, he had a total of seven diagnoses. Seriously? *Seven*? I had gone from wanting to know where we fit to fitting into so many places that absolutely nowhere felt right anymore! The moms of cookie-cutter autism kids had their support groups. The SPD moms could talk about where to get clothes with no tags and how they felt that people thought they were crazy when their kids had on shorts in mid-November. I was jealous of the ADHD moms, who had medications, such as Concerta, as an option. The moms of cognitively impaired kids seemed to be in their own group. I couldn't find my clique, and the friends I'd had my entire life clearly had no clue about what I was going through.

During this identity crisis, I felt resentful, annoyed, angry, sad, and, most of all, lost! I was wandering around like the lost little bird from the children's book *Are You My Mother?* I was desperate to find a soft spot to land.

When I was with moms of neurotypical kids, I would feel a constant need to explain. I spent a ton of time explaining to others what was "wrong" with Liam. I would blurt out way too much information out of fear that they were judging me, my parenting, or, the very worst, my child. Looking back on it, they were probably more curious about what was wrong with me, considering all the oversharing and overexplaining I did.

At one time in my life, I would have looked back and cringed at the thought of the incessant diarrhea of the mouth I had. Today, however, I am proud of the progress I have made. Recently I was out to lunch with a lifelong friend, and we both had our children with us. The waitress asked what we would like to drink, and Liam announced in the sweetest, most enthusiastic voice, "I love George Washington." (Liam tends to blurt out random words that are completely irrelevant to the situation.) It felt so good to just smile, say, "I know you do, buddy," and then tell the waitress that I'd love an iced tea.

So you are probably still waiting for me to tell you when you know you are a zebra, and here's what I am going to tell you: I am pretty sure the zebras aren't in the field counting each other's black stripes and white stripes. They aren't trying to determine if one has more horizontal stripes than the other. They are just sticking together, knowing they don't look like horses but that they are just as beautiful, strong, and resilient as any horse will ever be. They aren't thinking about whether they'd rather be horses because they are, in fact, zebras.

After I accepted that I am a zebra, I decided to learn more about this special animal. What I found out is that a zebra is a pretty awesome kind of animal to be. It is actually, in a lot of ways, like parents of children with special needs. Consider the following: A zebra's stripes are as unique as fingerprints—no two are exactly alike. However, each species has its own general pattern. Sound familiar? Also, zebras are social animals that spend time in herds; they want to fit in too! In fact, they are safest when they are in a group and weakest when they are singled out. If a zebra is attacked, its family will come to its defense, circling the wounded zebra and attempting to drive off predators. I know I welcome that kind of solid backup!

So what I am saying is embrace the herd. Most parents of kids with special needs are not looking to interview you for potential membership. They aren't going to ask for your membership card or care if you are a SPD parent or an ASD parent. As I am sure you have already learned, very few special-needs kids have just one diagnosis. Many kids on the autism spectrum also have sensory issues, and most kids with early onset bipolar disorder also meet the criteria for ADHD. Children with cognitive impairment may have autism as well. Because of these overlaps, we have so much we can learn from one another. We are each other's best resource, and sometimes, it's just nice to look across the field and know someone else gets what it's like to be a zebra!

Chapter 2

The Beginning of the Beginning

Oh my gosh, the beginning of the beginning! Although the beginning starts with the birth of your child, or maybe even before that, the birth is certainly a new beginning. From the moment of his birth, I feel as though I've had so many beginnings with Liam, and I have a feeling his life will be an assortment of beginnings. There was the beginning when I realized there was something different about my angel. There was the beginning of involving professional people who were *supposed* to know more about what was going on with him than I did. There was the beginning of our first plan. There was the beginning of doubting there was anything wrong in the first place, and then there was the beginning of diving in again, trusting my instincts, and feeling empowered to start anew.

I could seriously sit here and list dozens of beginnings, but I don't look at that as a lack of progress. I actually look at each new beginning as the ending of something that was no longer serving Liam or our family. Endings aren't necessarily bad or sad; they just signify that whatever was occurring has run its course. Each beginning has a new energy, attitude, idea, or plan. I think if I didn't experience each chapter in this journey as a new beginning, I would have curled up into a ball a long time ago.

Heck, there *were* times I did curl up into a ball! Nonetheless, that was the beginning of me accepting a new reality or circumstance. My dad told me a long time ago, "Kid, it's OK to lie down and lick your wounds; the problem is when you don't get back up." Beginnings are redos or start overs. Sometimes beginnings are just taking a shower or brushing our teeth, but we are, in fact, beginning something important or relevant every single day that we advocate for our children. Be patient with yourself! You are doing an amazing job at navigating through each and every beginning. So, if you curl up today, just begin again tomorrow.

The very beginning starts the moment you decide you are going to be a mother or father. It is like entering into an arena of the unknown, and so many emotions are conjured up. Whether the arrival of your child was planned, unplanned, adopted, or birthed, as a parent of a special-needs child you are beginning the journey of a lifetime, and there is no life raft! You are going to take in a lot of water, go under sometimes, and every now and then struggle to come up for air. There will be points when the turbulence is too great to fight against, and you will learn to go with the current. On occasion you will just float along, enjoying the scenery and taking in the beauty of it all. But the scenery will look different depending on your vantage point.

As the parent of a special-needs (atypical) child, there will be times you'll see your friends with non-special-needs (neurotypical) children hanging out on the bank, enjoying a whole different kind of journey, and you'll wonder why your experience can't be more like theirs. You'll feel bad for thinking it and probably not say it out loud for a long time, but believe me; you'll feel it. It's OK to feel it, and it's OK to say it out loud. That's what fellow zebras are for.

Having a fellow zebra is such a gift! You'll find you can say things to them that you'd never say to anyone else, and they will get it. You will laugh at things neurotypical parents would find appalling, and you'll have to give much less of an explanation!

People will tell you how amazing and strong you are for taking on such an uncertain path, and sometimes you will feel angry because it's not like you were given the choice. But I am here to promise you that *you* may not have chosen this path but *you* were *certainly chosen* for it! My sister reminds me of this time and again, and often it is the one thing I need to hear. I joke all the time that I am overqualified and underperforming every single day! Heck, I am a nurse and a teacher, so shouldn't I have all my ducks in a row? Regardless, being Liam's *mom* is the only qualification that counts when it comes to giving him the life he was meant to have. Special-needs parents are up for the challenge—we have to be!

So my beginning with Liam was full of love, excitement, joy, and a whole lot of uncertainty. I love Liam in a way that I couldn't have possibly conceived before I became a mother. Until this day, I still find it difficult to believe my parents could possibly love me the way I love Liam and his little sister, Mira. But, like all new mothers, there were times I worried about the ways he behaved.

Of course, there were the normal colds that I would convince myself were pneumonia or persistent fevers that in my mind were most certainly typhoid. However, with Liam, it wasn't so much the typical worries that I pondered late at night. It was those things that everyone would brush off or tell me I was just being a "new mom" about and not to worry.

He was so hot all the time! His crib would be soaking wet from sweat shortly after he fell asleep, if we were *able* to get him to sleep. When I'd set him down, he'd go into a sheer panic, flailing his arms and legs and crying in a way that just seemed different to me. He'd cry if he heard a Weedwacker three doors down, and on his first birthday he was hysterical when everyone sang the traditional "Happy Birthday." Even today, when I watch the video footage of that day, I cry. I see the horror on his face and Liam trying to escape what would have been such an ordinary experience for others.

As the years passed, in many ways, Liam seemed like every other American kid. He loved the park, trucks, and McDonald's. But then there were those quirky things that I couldn't quite figure out. He would cover his ears when we'd walk down the street and cry in distress if we went on the expressway. Escalators were out of the question. Certain clothing could put him into a tailspin, and many days he would vomit from a mere attempt at brushing his teeth.

He had the most adorable voice I'd ever heard, but over time I realized that when he would speak to others, they'd look at me to translate what he had said. We put him into speech therapy, and I thought maybe this was why he would sometimes get so overly frustrated. Maybe he was trying to express himself and was angered by how difficult it was. Then again, even when we did understand him, his reaction to things never seemed to quite match the stimulus. I said that so many times! I would just be baffled at how crushed or furious he would get about something that would be no big deal to other children. I would tell my mom that it was as if he were absolutely heartbroken. It felt as if I were trying to put together a puzzle that had mismatched pieces.

I struggled with whether or not to send Liam to preschool, but my parents had always told me it was a parent's job to teach his or her children to fly. As difficult as it was, I believed this too and wanted to give Liam every opportunity to become exactly who he was meant to be. So off to preschool he went, and although he was very shy with the children, he didn't mind going.

Liam was bright beyond his years and insightful like you'd never expect from a young child. He loved to share his ideas, and he talked a lot about them. His preschool teacher brought to our attention that sometimes he would tell her "it doesn't seem like the real world is real," and he shared many nightmares with her. I was aware of both of these things, but who do you call when your child tells you he's having "that feeling" and that "things don't seem real"? "Kids say funny things," people would tell me, and so I just put that puzzle piece in the box.

Liam made it through two years of preschool, had a few friends, and came into his own. We became accustomed to his little quirks and got used to tucking his pajama bottoms into his socks because he hated it when they pulled up in bed. I learned where I could buy clothing that fit just right and believed with all my heart that there was nothing good to come from forcing him to wear things that made his skin crawl. I bought gun-range muffs for him to wear to local parades and learned very quickly that going to the movies was way too much for him to handle.

I looked at things in a different way because of my little angel, and this new way became our normal. As for Liam's extreme reactions to things—his inability to cope with a change in the schedule or hours of crying following a simple request to come to lunch when he wanted to complete a painting—I thought if I just kept reading and trying new parenting techniques, I'd finally get it right.

Kindergarten isn't what it used to be. Gone are the days of cutting and pasting. The expectations are very high for these little people, and this was when I really started to worry about my sweet buddy. According to his teacher, he was doing everything he could "just to keep it together" during the school day. However, when he got home, it was like he'd release all his pent-up feelings on me. He was irritable, angry, and often inconsolable. He would panic if I mentioned a possible run to the store. It got to where I didn't go anywhere with him, and I'd try to get all my running around done with his little sister, Mira, while he was at school. His teacher suggested we have him evaluated.

Where does one go to have "quirky" evaluated? Herein lies where another beginning began! This was when we were introduced to the many recipes for alphabet soup: AS (Asperger's syndrome), now referred to as ASD (autism spectrum disorder); ADHD (attention deficit hyperactivity disorder); OCD (obsessive-compulsive disorder); SPD (sensory processing disorder); EOBP (early onset bipolar disorder); AD (articulation disorder); and LD (learning disabled). These were all diagnoses from the study of pediatric neurodevelopment, all letters that made me feel as if I couldn't breathe, all letters that have helped me help him.

We can't fear beginnings. We have to embrace them, acknowledge the gift in this new start, and then move forward. The current *is* going to keep moving. The shoreline is going to keep passing us by. It is up to us what we do along the way. We can fight the current tooth and nail, or we can learn to use it to our advantage. We can ignore the beautiful scenery, or we can enjoy the downtime and take it all in.

There will be plenty of life rafts to hang on to along the way; it is up to us to take the help. There will be people who want to jump into the water to assist, and there will be people who don't even know how to swim themselves. We can learn a lot from them all, if we take the time to hear what they have to offer. I do know it is much less lonely to go on the journey with others who care about us and our children than to bravely go it alone. You will be surprised by how much knowledge and compassion people have to share. You will just have to take a leap of faith and put out a hand in your time of need.

Chapter 3

Maybe It's Me? Maybe I Just Suck!

In my head, where I think many things I wouldn't dare say out loud, I thought to myself, which day is the day I decide my child is different enough that I need to tell someone else? The thought felt like a betrayal, like I was a horrible mother betraying my son. Who thinks this about his or her child? Maybe it's just me? I wondered. There were days I prayed it was just me!

There were so many days when it was just him and me alone at home, and I would convince myself everything was just "perfectly normal." Then there were days I would stare and wonder and fear there was actually something truly wrong with Liam. Then there were also days I was completely OK with thinking he was "perfectly quirky." I think the perfectly quirky days were my favorites, because they were a beautiful balance of my reality. Quirky put my mind at ease, and to me he was perfectly Liam!

Nonetheless, the doubts and worries never stayed away long, and neither did the guilt of having doubts and worries. This was the beginning of collecting all of the puzzle pieces that make up my sweet Liam. What I didn't realize at the time was all the growth *I* was being forced to make as well. Many of the puzzle pieces needed their own bag labeled "Kelly's Pieces," but it was some time before I realized that.

I have always been a person who likes approval. I did well in school, followed the rules, and hated to disappoint my parents. I snuck out of the house only once as a teenager, and even then I left a note in case my folks woke up! I am not kidding—I left a note explaining I had snuck out but would be back soon. I didn't like it when people seemed less than approving, so I did my best to always earn approval.

Fast-forward to my adulthood and all the judgment that comes along with parenting; as you can imagine, this was a pretty uncomfortable place for me! There were opinions from the get-go: to circumcise or not to circumcise, breastfeed or formula, co-sleep or crib from the start? So many theories, so many opinions, and I was in charge of picking what felt right for me. Ugh! There were days I wanted to run away, shut out the world, and cocoon up with my little guy. The thing is these are tough decisions to come up against for any new mom or dad, but couple it with having a special-needs kiddo, and you just multiplied the confusing issues by a zillion!

For me, I didn't know off the bat that Liam had special needs. I just thought I sucked at parenting. Not even kidding! I couldn't get him to sleep to save my life. People would explain how I should let him cry it out. If I set him down, he would go into a sheer panic, but enthusiastic helpers would explain his reaction showed the poor darling was getting spoiled.

Although I was a committed breastfeeding mom, when I went back to work for a short stint, I thought he would finally learn to take a bottle. Twelve to thirteen hours I'd be gone, and that little baby wouldn't take a sip! He would cry and wail and refuse to take one single ounce from that bottle. People would pooh-pooh me and say, "If he's really hungry, he'll eat."

I like to think I am a smart person. I graduated with honors from two colleges with two degrees, both pertaining to children's health and development. Yet I hung on to other people's words like they were oxygen, disregarding all that I knew. I don't mean just what I knew from college. I mean what I knew as a mother—Liam's mother! I knew something was off. I knew something didn't seem right. Since my journey wasn't following the path of those before me, I knew it must be something *I* was or wasn't doing.

As the years went by, my concern grew deeper, and although I couldn't put my finger on it, I knew we were going down a road less traveled. Liam's kindergarten teacher, Mrs. Brooks, gave me the courage to have him evaluated, and there we were at another beginning. I finally said it out loud. I told someone with letters after his name that I was concerned about my son. I didn't get the answers I had hoped for, but it was a beginning.

My skin has gotten so incredibly thick since then. I have learned a balance between appreciating others' input while still using my intuition to make decisions. I had no idea how crucially important this balance was going to be for my survival, but I certainly do now! I have had to advocate for Liam, Mira, and myself. I have had to learn to believe in myself and my instincts. I have learned that the most important approval of all is my own.

Yes, there are days we fall short. We don't stick to a recommended therapy program or can't enforce the behavior plan for one more minute. There are days we still worry that people are judging us or our children. However, look at it like this: our report card may not be full of shining stars, but we took the AP classes! We took on the biggest challenge, and in the end, we will reap the biggest reward. We are learning and loving and growing every single day of our lives. There is no better report card than that, and *no*! We don't suck!

Chapter 4

Do I Have Munchausen Syndrome?

One day I was in a doctor's office for one of Liam's many appointments, and I actually asked this question. Munchausen syndrome is a mental disorder where a parent, usually the mother, makes others believe that his or her child is sick. Some individuals are so mentally ill that they will do things, such as put toxic additives in the child's food, to actually make the child physically ill.

When I asked the doctor this question, he actually started laughing. I asked why he was laughing, and he said people who have Munchausen syndrome don't ask if they have it. OK, I thought, I guess this is good news; it sounds like I don't have it. But then he went on to say that he didn't think I had it but he could see how, if someone didn't know me better, someone may think I did.

Wow, what do you say to that? As I mentioned earlier, gaining approval was my big thing, so this felt *really* uncomfortable. Since I doubted myself enough on a daily basis, I certainly didn't need someone who was supposed to be helping me put the puzzle together seem to doubt me too. I was angry, sad, frustrated, and embarrassed. If he thought this about me, how many other people were thinking the same thing?

The situation was so hard because I wasn't even completely sure what was wrong with my little buddy. There were days I couldn't even sum it up in my own head. I didn't even know what was normal anymore! How on earth was I going to articulate to others what was going on?

This was an extraordinarily isolating feeling. I felt like I either didn't want to talk about Liam at all or the polar opposite, like I was going to do a seminar about his struggles every time someone merely asked how the kids were doing.

This dilemma goes back to that identity crisis: my identity and Liam's identity. I desperately wanted answers and concrete explanations. I wanted Liam's struggles wrapped up with a pretty bow so I could seamlessly explain to others that A, B, C, here's the story, thank you very much. It was hard enough navigating my own emotions during these early stages; I didn't have the time or energy to convince others of what was going on. This complexity was particularly difficult with extended family, which I will go into later.

So the appointment with this doctor was one of those gifts I told you about earlier. A ton was revealed from this experience. It took months, maybe even years, for it to be completely revealed, but it has, nonetheless, been a gift. What I learned is that each person who comes into our lives serves some sort of purpose. A person who questions us ultimately encourages us to rethink our stance or opinion. A person who supports us may increase our confidence when we are full of doubt. An individual who easily gives up may inspire us to try even harder.

I believe we need people in our lives who can act as a yin to our yang. Yin and yang can be thought of as complementary forces. We don't want to surround ourselves with yes-men but, more so, people who balance us. I learned I needed to recruit people to be part of a common goal. I call it Team Liam, and you can't be on the team unless you want to learn more about or contribute to helping Liam become the very best Liam he can be.

I am always looking for out-of-the-box thinkers who are going to ask questions, challenge data, and be proactive with the conclusions. However, members can't bring negative energy that is going to breed doubt and insecurities. We need different team members for different reasons. I might find a neurologist who is brilliant but has zero bedside manner. That is OK if we have another team member who can help us process the emotional piece of the data presented by the neurologist.

We need people who will not only advocate for our child but will advocate for our family. If we are going over the deep end, it is crucial that someone on the team will be there to either call us out or keep us from falling. Sometimes we will need someone to balance us out, and that isn't a bad thing—it is a gift. New energy and new perspectives are good things as long as team members are supportive and respectful of the very long journey we have already been on and understand that this life with a special-needs child is *our* 24/7.

Being in the thick of it, sometimes you feel like there is no air left to breathe. This is when it's OK to take a step back, regroup, and begin again by reassessing those surrounding you and how their energy affects you. If a person is bringing something to the table, then great! But if a team member is taking more energy than he or she is giving, then it is more than fair to reassess if that person is in tune with our common goal.

I stopped taking Liam to that doctor. I am not going to lie; on occasion I have wanted to send him a note to declare I wasn't crazy. In my most insecure moments, I have thought that sending him a list of Liam's very authentic diagnoses would somehow be productive, but I haven't! How's that for growth?

I have come so far from those early days of wondering if I had Munchausen syndrome. Now, when I think back to that time, I realize that I really wished I did have Munchausen, because that would be *my* burden instead of Liam's. Even at the beginning, I was hoping it was me, because then it wouldn't have to be him. Isn't that what being a parent is all about—being willing to take on any burden to prevent your child from experiencing pain?

Chapter 5

What Do Seven Diagnoses Look Like When You Put Them in a Blender?

When Liam was in first grade, we had a formal meeting to have him officially qualified for special-education services. One of the people at the meeting, who had gotten to know Liam quite well, described him as a mosaic. That description has always stuck with me. It is a beautiful way of saying Liam is complex, yet beautiful. Much like a mosaic, if you look too closely at Liam, you won't see the whole picture. Yet it is crucial to consider each one of Liam's diagnoses separately to help you understand how each piece interacts with the others.

I am a visual person, so when I picture Liam's diagnoses, I picture each disorder in its own Hula-Hoop but with frequent overlapping of those hoops, a Venn diagram of sorts but with fluidity, where the circles ebb and flow. Sometimes the diagnoses barely cross paths, and at other times, they are directly on top of each other.

Sometimes Liam's diagnoses are like oil and water. Other times, symptoms of one disorder are like fuel on fire to another disorder. If Liam is already feeling overwhelmed because his sensory system is overloaded due to his SPD, and then I give him a reminder that he needs to be off the computer in five minutes, which requires the ability to transition, a hallmark weakness for people with ASD, he may completely lose it. The agitation that is inherent with sensory overload, coupled with Liam's inability to transition, compromises his coping skills.

So what do compromised coping skills look like? Oh, there are a plethora of possibilities, depending on where his mood is at due to his bipolar disorder and how neurotically obsessed Liam is with the computer at the moment, reflective of his OCD. He may yell and throw pillows, venting his frustration like a teapot whistling out excess steam, or he may flip the entire coffee table while spewing out horrible obscenities, like an exploding volcano.

If you walked into the room while Liam was having an "episode," which is my preferred term for Liam's inability to cope, you might think he was an out-of-control brat who was having an obnoxious tantrum. However, it is much more like an emotional seizure, where the circuits in Liam's brain are malfunctioning so tragically that he loses complete control of the reasoning centers of his brain. The reasoning centers literally shut down, and until they are back up and running, Liam is no longer in control. We have named this bossy brain, and when bossy brain is in control, look out!

To say Liam's level of stability is variable is an understatement. When the stars are all aligned, he appears to be borderline typical with some quirky sprinkled in. He can socialize with other children, and from afar, you may not even guess he has special needs. However, the possibility for him to destabilize is always right over the horizon, and that truth keeps this momma on high alert.

Liam's autism would be relatively high functioning if it existed in a vacuum. Although he does struggle with flexibility, transitions, and comprehending that other people have a different perspective than his, he, surprisingly, has a good sense of humor, is affectionate at times, and sometimes experiences empathy, all of which are normally difficult for people with ASD.

That being said, when Liam has a multitude of stressors assaulting him at once, it can go south very quickly. I liken Liam to a darkened, two-liter bottle that you can't see through. You never know how full he is, meaning what level of functioning he is at, so you never know if he is about to overflow. So if his bottle is near empty, he may be able to tolerate music playing in the car while Mira and I discuss options of what we will do when we arrive home. His bottle has room for this kind of input. However, if he has been overheated all day, already has a plan in his head about what he wants to do (which happens often), and he has been feeling generally agitated most of the day, Mira and I merely singing and chatting about plans could be a recipe for disaster.

When Liam's at his most unstable, when we just can't seem to get his medications to help him function, episodes can be terrifying, and we call these rages. It is no exaggeration to say there have been weeks I have spent in excess of eight to ten hours having to restrain Liam on the floor to prevent him from damaging property, hurting himself, or hurting others. It's as though he is having a physical panic attack as a result of a seemingly benign circumstance, and once that runaway freight train starts down the tracks, all we can do is wait for it to run out of steam.

I often joke that if God was going to give me an autistic, bipolar child who has multiple other diagnoses, couldn't he have made him small? At only eleven years of age, Liam already weighed in at 140 pounds, was five foot five inches tall, and wore a men's size-eleven shoe. The strength he possesses during his rages is extraordinary and can be devastating. He has kicked through the drywall more times than I can count, thrown heavy counter stools with ease, and even kicked his bare foot through a double-pane window.

Even more devastating than the physical trauma is the emotional toll these episodes take on all of us. Mira has witnessed horrific scenes with her brother verbally threatening to kill all of us, or himself, while adults hold him down to prevent further devastation. As his mother, I know I am doing whatever I must to keep my children safe; nonetheless, it is absolutely beyond comprehension and gut-wrenching to be in this nightmare with your children.

For Liam, my heart crumbles each and every time he comes out of the fog, realizing what has occurred and not fully understanding why. He hates himself for the desolation he has caused, and his feelings of guilt can be insurmountable. On many occasions he has screamed that he just wants to die, so he doesn't have to experience the unrelenting episodes and the aftermath. Liam has literally begged me to kill him or for me to let him kill himself. These are words that will make a parent unable to breathe, consumed with fear and horror, knowing what their precious child is forced to endure.

I know I am biased, but Liam is the bravest child I have ever encountered! He perseveres through the unimaginable and wakes up to start anew each morning. He can be in agony midafternoon and then work his way back to childhood by evening. He looks for meaning in why all of this has been part of his journey and ponders concepts beyond his years. I am so proud to be his mother, and I always promise him that together there's nothing we can't get through. I will never stop fighting for my sweet angel; for me, that is just *not* an option!

Chapter 6

Candlelit Dinners While Raising a Child with Special Needs—Is That an Oxymoron?

I have spent time married and I have spent time single during my journey as a special-needs mother. One thing I can say for sure is that either scenario requires tenacity and a sense of humor, if nothing else! My mom told me a long time ago that sometimes relationships require a lot of effort. Well, she was spot-on with that statement, and that statement wasn't factoring in my special-needs world.

I met my children's father, Bill, when we were twenty-four years old. We got married at twenty-six, and I was pregnant by twenty-nine. I was very idealistic and had images of a white picket fence and a happily ever after in my mind for sure! I think back to that very young woman and I love her for her ability to have hope, even when there wasn't a whole lot to hang her hat on. We were financially struggling, like many young couples, in debt with Bill's law-school loans, and overwhelmed with both of us starting new careers. I truly believed that none of that mattered because, at the end of the day, we had love.

Liam's birth was much planned. I still have the budget we made to make sure we'd be able to make ends meet with a new family member. We were overjoyed when we found out on New Year's Eve that I was pregnant, and we couldn't wait to tell our families the exciting news. I continued to have hopeful energy that everything was going to be wonderful, and, in many ways, it was.

Liam was born in September of 2002, full-term and just perfect. He did have a quick stay in the neonatal unit for monitoring because I had a fever during labor. Otherwise, the only thing that sticks out in my mind about his birth is the neonatologist coming to speak with us about Liam's head circumference. He wanted to make sure we kept an eye on the fact that Liam's weight and height were both above the ninetieth percentile, while his head was only in the tenth. Being a pediatric nurse, this raised all kinds of questions from me, but he assured us it was just something to keep an eye on, so we did.

I think we both took to parenting pretty naturally. We never saw the lifestyle change as a hindrance; staying home with our little guy was just fine with us. However, by the time Liam was one year old and still never sleeping for an extended period, I was beyond exhausted and felt like I was inept at getting him on a schedule.

This was a very difficult time for me emotionally, but it was also very difficult on our marriage. We never seemed to go to bed at the same time, and I built up resentment that Bill got to sleep while I was endlessly struggling with a baby who wouldn't! I know he was frustrated too, and neither of us knew how to resolve the issue. There seemed to be a lot of blaming one another and no solutions.

Looking back at that time, I'm not sure I could have done anything differently regarding Liam's inability to sleep. I know I tried everything possible to get him to sleep, and nothing worked. The angle I never took, however, was, "How can I help *myself*?" What could I have done to make my situation more bearable? Maybe if I had reached out more for help from others, asking someone to take him during the day so I could sleep or to keep him overnight, I would have been more emotionally stable.

Deep down I was embarrassed that something as simple as a sleep schedule was beyond my capability. I was soooo sick and tired of everyone's advice, so I decided to go it alone. Had I known then what I know now—that bipolar children have an extraordinarily difficult time with sleep and most of them eventually end up on medication to help with this symptom of their disorder—maybe I wouldn't have felt so inept, embarrassed, and isolated. What I do know is that this was a wedge that pushed Bill and me apart, even though I did everything I knew how to fix the problem. It was a symptom of having a special-needs child when we didn't even know he had special needs.

Over the years, Bill and I have been in sync in a lot of ways regarding Liam's struggles. We both recognized before anyone else that something was atypical about our angel. I know that often the mother is on an island, either being the one to propel the diagnostic testing forward without support from her partner or being blamed for the child's struggles altogether. Liam's dad was on board, innately knowing, just as I did, that we needed to look into the possibilities regarding Liam's developmental progress.

Although we never fought about Liam's specific diagnoses, married life with a special-needs child can still be quite brutal. My experience as a wife and mother was spent as a stay-at-home mom. I often joke that I am overqualified and underperforming, and although I say I am joking, I know deep down in some ways I am acknowledging how I truly feel. I used to cry to Bill, saying he got a paycheck or kudos at work for his job well done, but at the end of the day my report card was a great, big *fail*! Even though Bill believed in Liam's diagnoses, I still felt so much responsibility for my child's struggles and lack of progress. After all, I was his mother, and I had left my careers to stay at home with our son. I no longer had a paycheck or a 401(k) to legitimize my contribution or success. I felt Liam's progress, or lack thereof, was the only evidence of my accomplishments.

Oftentimes I felt my time was spent spinning my wheels and having little or nothing to show for my efforts at the end of the day. I was doing everything I could possibly think of to create successful days for both of the children. Still, no matter how hard I tried, I always felt like I was falling short. I'd spend hours making schedules and activities for the kids. I found games that would entertain Mira while helping Liam with skills he so desperately needed. I'd have hope each morning, but usually by lunchtime I'd feel defeated and alone.

In a lot of ways, I envied Bill. I couldn't imagine what it would be like to shower in peace, leave for the day, and take a lunch break whenever it fit into my afternoon. I envied how he could actually complete a project at work and have a finished product that he could hang his hat on! My finished product felt so intangible, and I resented that he had one, and I didn't.

The crazy thing is although I resented him for having what I perceived as the easier job, I wouldn't have traded mine for anything. I cherished every single moment I had with the kids, and when he would say, "Why don't you go back to work, and I'll stay home?" I'd feel protective of my role, like a mama bear! I knew I wanted to be the one in the trenches, but at the same time I felt desperate to have a report card that reflected my effort, commitment, and exhaustion. I think, at the end of the day, I needed him to give me verbal affirmation that I was doing an amazing job, because the evidence didn't often concur.

Bill shared with me many times that, even though he was at work, he thought of us constantly, worried sick about how Liam was doing. Was he being aggressive and hurting Mira or me? Why wasn't I answering the phone? He said it was difficult to be "on" at work when he was distracted by his thoughts that had wandered back home.

Needless to say, we were both tapped out much of the time and had pent-up anxiety and frustration about our reality. It wasn't exactly a recipe for candlelit dinners and great conversation. I regularly felt overstimulated by the end of the day; I was ready to shut down and curl up, needing to recharge for another round. We coped very differently with our stress, and this certainly created a wedge between us.

Someone once explained to me what our relationship was mimicking. She said it was as if we were both drowning, and neither one of us had a life jacket. We each could barely tread water long enough to keep ourselves afloat, let alone offer assistance to the other. We were desperately exhausted and looking to each other for help! How can you save someone else from drowning when you are almost drowning yourself?

The upside was we both understood what it was like to be drowning. We could relate in a lot of ways. We were the only two parents to these miraculous human beings; we understood the glory and the pain like no one else could. We can still look across the room and not have to say a word, because we know realities that no one else can possibly know. I believe that connection will outlast our hardest days. I believe, even in heartache, there can be gifts, and that is one I plan on cherishing, because it's not something that can be re-created.

When people find out Bill and I are divorced, they are always quick to assume it was a result of our raising a special-needs child. I am quick to say that wasn't our demise, but I guess every chapter makes up a book, and that part was a very significant chapter. I tend to look at it as we grew together in a ton of ways because of our special-needs child, and conversely, we grew apart in a ton of ways too. I don't believe you can hang your hat on one single thing when it comes to a marriage ending. However, when you decide parting ways is the best decision, you are forced to begin writing the next chapter.

Chapter 7

I Am a Boiling Frog

The boiling-frog theory is actually pretty grotesque. Still, I have referred to this theory when describing my life on countless occasions. I think the story is about as accurate as it gets when trying to explain to another person how I am able to continue getting up and showering (most days) in spite of the chaos that often surrounds me.

The theory goes something like this:

Apparently, if you gently put a frog in a pot of tepid water and then slowly turn up the temperature, you can boil it alive. Supposedly, the frog will never jump out of the pot, because it acclimates to the temperature as the temperature gradually increases, and, therefore, the frog never hits a threshold where it knows to leap out to protect itself.

I often say I am a boiling frog. Some days I thank God I am a boiling frog, because I am pretty sure if you just dropped me suddenly in the boiling pot of my life, I would most certainly jump out. I am grateful life has gradually immersed me into my reality, because it has given me time to gain perspective and knowledge, both attributes that are crucially necessary for the marathon of raising a child with special needs. I can remember a time when the idea of Liam possibly having special needs was more than I thought I could bear. I wish I knew then how strong I would become and the person I would evolve into along the way.

If you had told me when Liam was two that his tenth birthday would be spent at an inpatient pediatric psychiatric facility, I would have thought you were sick and twisted, especially if you had added that my mother would be sleeping there, doing one of the night shifts, when I arrived to tell her that her own mother had died. If you had told me that I would eventually buy a metal safe for storing all sharp objects, including my kitchen scissors, I would have thought you were more likely describing a tragic scene from a movie. If you had told me that over a two-year period Liam would spend a total of fifteen weeks in the hospital, I think I would have stopped breathing at the mere thought.

I am a boiling frog. It is what has made it possible for me to shower. It has made it possible for me to still go to lunch with my girlfriends, to work in Mira's classroom for the holiday party, or to make small talk when I run into an old friend. I have slowly acclimated to my reality. I think that's what most parents of children with special needs do. Being a boiling frog has bought me the time I need to reassess, regroup, or just plain old get a grip.

The human mind is miraculous. It protects us when we otherwise can't protect ourselves. It has an amazing ability to help us accept a new truth. It's what gets people through the unthinkable. Those things that we think we could never endure, we can endure because of our minds' resolve.

One of my best friends growing up, and still a very close friend today, tragically lost her mother to cancer when we were only sixteen years old. I have learned so much from Karen over the many years of our friendship, but one was a profound lesson I am able to apply to my life during my toughest struggles.

When her mother first died, I looked at her in awe. I couldn't believe how "well" she got through it all. Finally one day I said to her, "I don't know how you're doing it. I could never get through losing my mom like you have." I said it as a compliment, but as a naïve, young woman, I didn't know just how insensitive it sounded.

She looked at me and said one of the most profound statements a person who has been through tragedy could say: "It's amazing what you can do when you don't have a choice." Wow, how spot-on she was!

I don't chalk my life up to a tragedy. I believe I have had way more gifts than struggles. But I do know it's amazing what we can get through when we don't have a choice. I wouldn't change my life, even if given the chance. I would take away Liam's pain, of course, but I wouldn't change how it's shaped who I've become. The strength, resolve, and commitment that have grown inside me as I have learned to advocate for all of us is more than I could have ever predicted. Being a boiling frog has kind of made me a badass of sorts, and I am proud to have survived the scorching heat!

Chapter 8

Please Don't Tell Me How to Get My Baby to Sleep: How Unwanted Advice Can Make Us Crazy!

I had Liam in a playgroup from the time he was three months old. We would line up the babies and take the most adorable pictures of them every month when we would meet at one of our homes for lunch and playtime. Most of the mothers I had known since childhood, and we couldn't believe we had all grown up, gotten married, and had children. We were living the dream. Those playdates were great outlets for adult conversation and gave all of us a reason to actually shower and get out of the house. It was such a comfortable group of safe women who supported one another as we navigated our way through early motherhood.

We each had our strengths, so it was great to know if I had a question about nursing, I could ask Andrea; if it was about budgeting, I could ask Jenny; and if it was about how to work in date night, I could ask Wendy. I was dubbed the organization guru, along with having a PhD in stain removal. There were about ten of us who rotated houses, and we watched each other's children grow up.

I have never been a keeping-up-with-the-Jones's type of gal, so when Liam was the last one to master rolling, sitting up, and walking in the group, I rolled with it. No problem. Being a nurse, I knew there was a range of normal, and I tended not to sweat the small stuff. He still refused to take milk unless he was nursing, but I brushed it off and figured this was a precious time in our lives and it would be over before I knew it.

But by the time the kids were reaching one year old, I was the only one who couldn't get a sleep schedule established. Heck, I couldn't get him to sleep at all unless I was snuggled up next to him or was holding him on the couch. I was tired and frustrated! I tried taking advice from one friend or another, but nothing seemed to work. I read books, searched online, and even ordered a DVD that promised to "make all your sleep problems disappear!" I felt as if I was failing, and I was exhausted while doing so!

This situation not only affected how long my nights became but it affected every part of my day. I was convinced I was the only person awake at such ungodly hours, and I felt so isolated! I was tired before I even got out of bed in the morning, and my first thought was always, "When can I sleep next?" Each day I would vow, "Today is going to be different! Today I am going to figure out how to make this child sleep!"

Now, when you haven't slept for longer than two hours at a time in over a year, you find yourself doing some irrational things. Ask any husband who throws away what he thinks is a piece of scrap paper only to later find out it was actually your child's precious first artistic creation. Exhausted moms aren't always at their most reasonable!

After another very long week without sleep, I once promised myself I wasn't going to pick up Liam from that crib! The book said if I picked up Liam, he'd know the crying worked. It was crucial that I not pick him up, so I didn't. The book did not, however, say I couldn't get into the crib with him!

Now, I know what you're thinking: that had to be dangerous, as I weigh too much to be in the crib with him. Nonetheless, in the midst of desperation, I was still able to make mathematical computations in my head. Liam's crib was one of those three-in-one cribs; it was designed to be a crib, toddler bed, and, eventually, an adult head and footboard. I reasoned that certainly it could hold my weight as it was designed to eventually hold two grown adults!

Bingo! Over the railing I went, and we both fell sound asleep. Desperate times call for desperate measures!

I think back, and this was the beginning of me feeling like I sucked. I can vividly remember being at a friend's house and her casually saying, "I'll be back in a minute. I'm going to put the baby down." When she literally returned in five minutes with no baby and turned on a monitor to nothing but the sound of a mobile playing, I was astonished! Oh my gosh! What on earth have I just witnessed? I thought to myself.

I couldn't even begin to imagine what kind of freedom that would bring! Don't get me wrong. I had learned to enjoy my time sitting there holding Liam. I would stare at his beautiful face and watch him breathe softly as he lay in my arms or next to me on the couch or bed. I would tell myself that this was a finite time in both of our lives and that this was just how it was. Still, the idea of setting Liam down without him screaming in sheer panic and actually showering—now there was something very appealing about that!

Like many things in life, if you haven't experienced it, you *can't* imagine what it's like to go through it. Having a child who doesn't sleep is one of those things. I think this was the first topic that could bring instant tears to my eyes and make me want to shoot daggers at anyone who made it sound like it was just so simple. I can remember being at a baby shower for my college roommate when a bunch of moms started talking about sleep schedules. I mentioned that Liam "just won't sleep," and I immediately had suggestion after suggestion on how to remedy my problem. Even when I would try to explain to them that I had tried all of their ideas and that he literally just *wouldn't* sleep, they would give me another sure way to make it so he would. I cried in the middle of the luncheon. I think it was as much because I was tired as it was that I felt so isolated. They just didn't get it or hear me! I wanted to scream, "What part of *won't sleep* are you people not getting?!"

Gosh, that feeling is awful! Just thinking about it makes my stomach ache. I've had that same feeling dozens of times about a laundry list of things since then, but today I have learned to deal with those moments in much healthier ways. I have learned that it's OK if people don't get it. Not everyone will. Actually, much of the time, the list of people who *don't* get your reality will be much longer than the list of people who do. That's just how it is. It doesn't mean you suck. It doesn't mean that you are crazy. It just means that you are experiencing parenthood in a different way from many of the people you know.

In the Alcoholics Anonymous and Al-Anon programs, there's a slogan: "Take what you like, and leave the rest." This simply points out to us that there is always value in what people have to share. You get to decide what that value is for you. Maybe someone will say something that will strike a chord. Maybe someone's suggestions will remind you of how much you have already tried. Maybe, by listening to someone, you will help that person feel valued. As parents supporting each other through the hardest, most worthwhile journey we will ever take, all we have to do is take what we like and leave the rest. If you find yourself in a battle of wills, insisting that someone see it from your point of view, you need to ask yourself, "What is the value in that?"

Chapter 9

When We Know Better, We Do Better

"Do the best you can until you know better. Then when you know better, do better." ~Maya Angelou

People usually just really want to help. However, I have learned that human beings are very uncomfortable watching another suffer or be in pain. They are uncomfortable with your discomfort, so they want your discomfort to go away. If you believe that most people are more good than bad, then you have to believe they don't know how much suffering their "helpfulness" is causing. They don't know their words are diminishing how you feel. They don't know that your challenge is much bigger than their small suggestions. They don't mean to cause us pain, so we need to cut them some slack. They just don't know.

Another thing I have learned is that people are usually doing the best that they can. When I was a young adult, my sister could be critical of the way I handled things. I would always tell her, "I am doing the best that I can!" She hated for me to say that because she thought it was a cop-out. Fast-forward through twenty years of life experience on both of our parts, and we now *both* believe this about people in general. We believe people don't wake up thinking, I am going to really try to suck today! We are all doing the best that we can with the tools that we have. When we don't have tools, we tend to use weapons. So what we need to do for personal growth is acquire more tools.

We need to take responsibility for ourselves and our reactions to other people's choices or words. If someone says something that is hurtful, or what we perceive to be insensitive, we get to decide what we do with that. I once had a therapist tell me that we are all 100 percent responsible for our portion. So, if you are in an argument with someone and you feel he or she is 80 percent wrong and you are only 20 percent wrong, you are still 100 percent responsible for your 20 percent. Initially I thought, *rip-off*! That person is way more at fault! But this theory about being 100 percent responsible for your portion is so true.

I really believe Maya Angelou's famous quote, "When we know better, we do better." So being honest with the people in our lives about how they are making us feel gives them the opportunity to do better. If they don't know that their words are hurting or frustrating us, they don't know to stop. Better yet, if we share with them what *is* helpful, they can do better the next time we need support.

So what are the tools we can use when people offer suggestions or perspectives that aren't helpful? We can say, "Thanks for sharing." We can take what we like and leave the rest. We can share with them that we know they are well intended and don't mean to hurt us, but when they say "X," it is frustrating, hurtful, or offensive. It might feel awkward at first, but I'd rather feel awkward for a moment than angry for a lifetime. We can tell them that we know it can be hard for them to watch us or our child struggle, and sometimes just acknowledging that fact will make it more comfortable for everyone involved.

Remember the girlfriend I mentioned earlier who lost her mother to cancer? Karen's precious mother died on the Ides of March (March 15). Every year since, on the eve of March 14, I call her to say I am thinking of her. Some years we barely discuss her mom, and other years she and I cry together about how difficult it has been for her—graduating from high school, getting married, and becoming a mother of three herself—without her beautiful, dedicated mother by her side. Some people have said it is odd that I call Karen like that. They think it just reminds her of a devastating topic.

What I know to be true is that on March 14, she knows it is the day before the anniversary of her mother's passing, whether I call or not. If I pretend it isn't happening, I am only diminishing her truth. Sometimes people are horribly uncomfortable standing silently by the side of pain or discomfort. Sometimes we have to invite them into that inner sanctum of our truth.

Once people know what you expect or need from them, their discomfort diminishes. I experienced this firsthand with my friends and family when I was going through infertility while trying to have Mira. I'd found out at thirty years of age that I had the eggs of a forty-five-year-old. My doctor told me I could keep trying for a healthy pregnancy but the odds were against me. I could get pregnant very easily, but I couldn't stay that way for long; usually, less than seven weeks along, I would lose the baby. Mira was our fifth try, and without a doubt, she is one heck of a good egg!

That period in my life was a long, dark, and painful road. I was hurting, angry, and confused, and I felt insufficient. It was heartbreaking. It was devastating. I didn't want people to say clichés or make suggestions, such as "keep a positive attitude." Once someone told me her niece put her feet up and was able to carry the baby to term. I went ballistic! It wasn't pretty. I screamed that I was pretty sure if the doctors thought putting my feet up was the solution, we would have tried that option *before* shoving cameras up into my uterus!

I was using weapons. Eventually, I shared with the people in my life that I usually just needed people to acknowledge that it sucked. My friend Andrea was always amazing at this type of response, and she was the first person I'd call after I lost yet another baby. She would sit on the other end of the phone and let me share, cry, and vent. She'd acknowledge that it was absolutely horrible and tell me she'd be by my side to get through it. I think sometimes people just need permission to agree with you when you say, "This is really awful!"

My point is to communicate. Share what you need. Tell people what is helpful, and tell them what is hurtful. Assume people are doing the best they know how with the tools that they have and that people just hate to see you and your child struggle. Fill up your toolbox, and put down your weapons. Be gracious, yet confident, and remember when we know better, we do better!

Chapter 10

I Wish There Was More I Could Do to Help!

Then there's the issue of people who are really serious about wanting to help you. How many times have people said to you, "Let me know if there's anything I can do," or "I wish I could be more helpful"? Let them! You will learn who really means it in no time! Tell those who offer what you actually need. Most people who offer really mean it, and it makes them feel empowered when you allow them to help. I have learned that if I am willing to accept it, support is everywhere. Below is a perfect example.

One Sunday I was having a surprise birthday dinner for my stepmom, Susanne, and I needed chocolate chips and vegetable oil to make her favorite: my famous chocolate-chip cookies. She is always one of my top supporters, so I just wanted to do something special for her. I had previewed with Liam that we'd be going to the store (not his strong suit to say the least!), and I had given myself plenty of time to accomplish my goal.

Well, sometimes (OK, usually) Liam is on his own program, and no matter how much I think I have things under control, it is really just an illusion. I finally got Liam into the car after forty-five minutes of chaos, only to have him refuse to actually come into the store. I pulled out all my tricks and was making absolutely no headway! I was frustrated, irritated, and felt incompetent. Seriously, all I needed to do was grab a few items from the store. Why couldn't I even accomplish that?

I live in a small village, kind of like something out of a Norman Rockwell painting, so I thought to myself, there's got to be someone going in or out of the store that I know. Now, a year before I would have had too much pride for this move, but after Liam had been hospitalized twice that year for a total of five weeks, I had gained much humility. I had learned to reach out. I had learned that I can't go it alone and that people don't want me to.

I took a deep breath and leaned against my minivan, scanning the parking lot. I knew it was my only hope, and I wasn't going to let down Mira or myself, as we were both looking forward to making a big batch of cookies for one of our favorite people. In less than five minutes, I saw a close friend walking out with her cart, and I felt my stress just disappear. I flagged her down, and without hesitation Andrea grabbed my list and ran back into the store, with Mira in tow, to grab my necessities!

My guess would be that if you asked Andrea, it made her feel good to help. She came back with my chocolate chips and oil and had even grabbed a bouquet of flowers as Mira had mentioned to her that we had talked earlier in the day about picking out some flowers for Zan. By the time they got back, Liam had calmed, I could breathe, and Mira felt like such a big girl for making our plan come to fruition.

Now, rewind the tape and play it out as if I had resisted seeking help. I am pretty sure I know what it would have looked like: I would have continued to try to coerce Liam into going inside the store. "Try" is the key word here because he had emotionally shut down before we even left the house and was to a point of being simply unable. My Pollyanna voice would have transitioned from supportive and encouraging to annoyed and disappointed. Mira would have been watching this all unfold and become, once again, resentful of Liam. We would have gone home all feeling defeated and disconnected, each of us blaming someone else for our disappointment.

Instead, I got a big hug from Andrea in the parking lot and was proud of myself for thinking outside the box. Liam calmed down, feeling glad that we could still go home and make the cookies, while Mira got to feel like the hero.

I followed up the trip with a text to my dear friend saying how grateful I am to have friends like her who make me feel safe enough to be vulnerable. It was a win for everyone! The dinner came off beautifully, and while the cookies baked, the kids made a big sign for Zan that we hung up for her arrival.

I think the key is looking at reaching out as being resourceful and not as failing. Your reality is your reality. We all have blessings, and we all have struggles. Accepting this fact and surrounding yourself with people who get your reality is key. I know I certainly don't have the time, energy, or interest in portraying to people that I've got it completely under control. The fact of the matter is I don't. I am pretty sure that if we were all honest, we'd learn none of us have it completely under control. We could all use a little support and backup, just like the zebras!

Interestingly enough, after asking for help a few times, it isn't nearly as scary as it seemed to be at the beginning. I think the scariest part is really admitting your truth, because when we say things out loud, they feel real! So the cat's out of the bag; now take a big breath and be proud of your truth. You are a survivor. You are going down the road less traveled, and the fact of the matter is that on this sometimes very lonely journey, the only way to survive is to reach out for help. I promise you often the result of you reaching out will be a bond or a strengthened relationship. At the very least, you'll have some funny stories about the silliest things for which you've asked for help!

Here are the ten oddest things for which I've sought help:

1.   Once I asked my stepmom, Susanne, "Will you please come over and help remove Liam from my leg? Mira has softball, and he is insisting that we are not going." When asked how soon I needed her, I said, "Three minutes ago!"

2.   To my girlfriend Dana I once requested, "Will you please buy a new water bottle for my guinea pigs and come over and put it in their cage? Ours is leaking, and I have to leave to take Liam to the hospital."

3.   There was a time when I asked a gentleman at Lowes, "Will you please push my cart out to the car for me so that I can walk alongside it? Sometimes my son jumps out and runs, and I need my hands free in case I need to grab him."

4.   I remember asking my friend and next-door neighbor Leah, "Will you please watch Mira for me? I am in your backyard, and Liam is trying to run away."

5.   There was also a time when I asked a saleswoman at a boutique on Mackinac Island, "Will you please put this stuffed dog on hold for me? If we buy it right now, my son will panic because he is afraid he doesn't want it, but if someone else buys it, he will panic because he is afraid he might want it."

6.   To a woman in a restaurant's bathroom, I once said, "Will you please hold off on flushing the toilet until my son is finished going to the bathroom? He is petrified of public toilets flushing."

7. Another time I asked Dana, "Will you please take my bags of recyclables? I can't get Liam out of the car, and he is using them as projectiles!"

8. I asked my friend and neighbor Don, "Will you please come over and help me empty my spare room? Liam has been really sensory seeking, so I am filling the room with padded material and beanbags."

9. One of my requests to Don and Leah was, "Can I borrow your shop vacuum? My son just kicked in a double-pane window during a rage, and I need to clean up the glass." (Thank God for neighbors who became great friends!)

10. I've also asked my neighbor and friend Evelyn, "Can Mira come down to your house for a while? I am restraining Liam and don't want her to have to sit here and watch me."

Chapter 11

You Will Get There When You Get There, and Not a Moment Too Soon!

There are so many ways of saying I should have done it differently: Monday morning quarterback, a day late and a dollar short, missed the boat, hindsight is twenty-twenty. It's a way to beat ourselves up for not doing it "right." Whether it's the time frame under which we came to a conclusion, the order in which we carried out a goal, or the mistake we accidentally made, as human beings we take great pride in beating ourselves up!

I once read that a key difference between our pets' and our own serenity is that we have the ability to rewind and play every single moment we've ever regretted. Have you ever seen your dog unsuccessfully try to catch a squirrel and then repeatedly bang his head against the side of your home? I am going with no on that! Fido just loops around, finds a sunny place to lounge, and promptly licks his parts! He has instantly moved on from the previous unsuccessful moment.

We, on the other hand, replay conversations in our heads and spend excessive time wondering about what things would be like if we had... We agonize over that one thing we missed or the thing we did that we never should have done. This is one of the most defeating human characteristics. There is a huge difference between obsessing over and dissecting our errors versus briefly considering what didn't work out in the past and how we can improve upon it in the future.

When we hyperfocus on our errors, we are spending an inordinate amount of time in the past. "Maybe if I had started her in physical therapy sooner," or, "I wonder what would have happened if I'd done a casein- and gluten-free diet from the get-go." These kinds of thoughts don't get us anywhere. You have to reframe your regrets in a way that can propel you forward in a healthy and positive direction. What's the old saying? If you have one foot in the past and one foot in the future, you're not standing in the present.

An example of this kind of regret for me is when I realized how long I sat and stared at Liam in complete turmoil during the fall of 2012. August had been a difficult month, as I watched Liam's agitation increasingly get worse. We could barely leave the house with him; Mira and I spent a ton of time cooped up, hoping for this period to pass. Over the next few weeks, he became stuck in a mixed state of mania and depression.

Mixed states are horribly difficult to stabilize. The mania causes Liam's energy level to be extraordinarily high. He has grandiose thinking and obsesses about things that are completely irrational. He's almost vibrating internally, and he tells me he can't stop the thoughts. The depressive portion increases Liam's agitation level even further, triggers negative and sometimes violent thoughts, and decreases his capacity to be any part of a solution. It's like watching him be sucked into an abyss as you helplessly stand by.

I knew full well that the slew of psychiatric and neurological medications he was on were not stabilizing him. By the first day of school, Liam was admitted to the pediatric inpatient psychiatric unit of a local university hospital. It was his first hospitalization, and I can't even put into words how grief stricken I felt. His stay lasted ten days, and upon discharge, there seemed to be some improvement.

I was excited for Liam's return home and kept my fingers crossed that the medications would help him function. My hope was short-lived, and by Thanksgiving it was evident the hospital stay, along with the discharge plan, had made very little forward progress for my sweet Liam. He was not much better than before he was hospitalized, and I watched as he actually slowly deteriorated week by week.

In no time it was a few weeks before Christmas, and I was doing everything I could to keep him out of the hospital for the holidays. By January 5, Liam had completely destabilized again. He was in the worst shape we had ever seen him in, up to that point, and he again ended up being admitted to the hospital, this time in Chicago and for twenty-three days. It was during one of those very long nights that it occurred to me, I had completely missed the boat! Why in the heck did I wait for so long to address the fact that his meds weren't working? What was I waiting for? Seriously, what was my problem? I fretted and beat myself up for not being more proactive. I blamed myself for him being hospitalized again and spent a ton of energy focusing on these thoughts.

Stop! Beating myself up was in no way, shape, or form going to change the past or the fact that Liam was hospitalized and as unstable as he'd ever been. Maybe changing his meds wouldn't have produced a different outcome. Maybe it would have made him worse. I will never know. What I do know is I now have a two-month rule regarding medication changes. If I don't see some kind of improvement in Liam's status, I make an appointment with his doctor to discuss what needs to happen next. Sometimes sitting and waiting has its benefits, but in this scenario, the potential downward spiral is too great a risk. If a medication is working, then I stay the course. If there is no result, or a slip backward happens, I am now way more proactive.

So I guess in a way I think it's appropriate to tap-dance in yesterday and tomorrow. I think it is imperative to learn from the past. The definition of insanity is doing the same behavior over and over while expecting a different outcome. So finding a happy medium between forgiving yourself for a job not so well done and being hypercritical of your shortcomings is crucial. As parents of special-needs kids, we always need to be reevaluating what's working and what's not. We sometimes need to make difficult or uncomfortable decisions because our reality has changed in a way that requires it.

This new way of framing my mistakes is a much more gentle way to treat myself. It's how I would treat my friend. It's giving myself the benefit of the doubt, full well knowing I did the best I could with what I knew at the time. Remember, as Maya Angelou said, "When we know better, we do better!"

Photographs

Photographs can be breathtaking, funny, emotional, thought provoking, startling, motivating, or misleading. They can instantly bring us back to a moment in time, good, bad, or otherwise. I couldn't believe how incredibly emotional it was for me to go through all of my photos for this book. I was flooded with such a huge mix of memories; it really stopped me in my tracks.

One thing that I absolutely took away from the photos is that, as a culture, we take great pride in capturing the happiest of moments. I have done an extraordinary job at teaching my children to put on a happy face for the camera, even when that expression is not remotely what they are feeling at the moment. This revelation certainly gave me pause, and I can't help but rethink how I will photograph them in the future.

The story that goes beyond the photo is what I find to be the truly fascinating piece. They say a picture speaks a thousand words, and sometimes I am sure this is the case. However, much of the time, a picture is only the catalyst for a conversation, delving into what is beyond the image. Below I am proud to share some of our moments, and I want to candidly let you into our truth beyond the lens.

I would bet there are thousands of pictures taken in front of this sign annually. Beyond the photos, there are thousands of different stories. For me this picture signifies the most tragic vacation of my life. The truth is Liam had his first episode of violent psychosis, losing complete touch with reality, while we were staying in a darling log cabin up in the mountains of Tennessee. It was so horrifying to watch, as his father lovingly restrained him, Liam spewing out words

I didn't even know he could utter. Two more such episodes occurred while we were there, and eventually, we sedated him to travel home, by recommendation of his psychiatrist.

Gun-range muffs have allowed us to participate in things we otherwise would have never been able to. I have several pair, and sometimes just Liam's knowledge that they are available alleviates his anxiety. This photo was taken at our local Fourth of July parade. We also take the muffs to the movies; the annual firemen's breakfast, in case someone turns on a siren; and to play laser tag. We spend time with people who understand Liam, and thankfully, no one has ever teased or made fun of him.

Sometimes I don't anticipate Liam needing his head-phones, and if he's not too overloaded, he will improvise. In this picture we are at a local petting farm and he is afraid the animals will make a loud, unexpected sound. I can't tell you how many times I have stood behind him, holding his ears tightly so he can breathe, public restroom included!

Over the years I have tried very hard to create one-on-one time with both of my kids. Mira's world has been atypical, to say the least, and I believe it is imperative for her to have experiences without her brother. Liam limits what we can do much of the time, and to see Mira flourish without boundaries is exceptional. In this photo we are at an indoor water park for unlimited Mira and Momma fun!

This photo always makes me chuckle. It was taken at the wedding of my friends Joan and Todd. The truth is I missed the ceremony because Liam was agitated, on the verge of having a meltdown. I left Mira in the church with my friend Dana, so Liam and I could go out into the huge parking lot and count Mini Coopers. He spent the entire time talking about how he wanted the first piece of cake. He clearly had *zero* perspective about how the cake symbolized a ton for those two people in the fancy outfits who were getting *married*. Amazingly, Joan gave it to him.

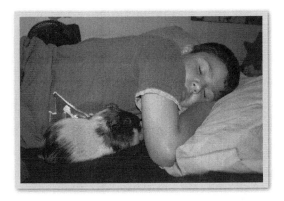

Liam's guinea pig, Jedi, has been a huge source of comfort for Liam! Mira will often bring Jedi to him when she can tell he is getting agitated. Many times Liam has fallen asleep while snuggling with Jedi, and not once has Jedi left his side. I am always amazed by Jedi's instinct to stay right by Liam. I truly have no idea how we will get through Jedi's passing. I dread it!

This photo was taken at the Autism Speaks walk in 2010. My girlfriends surprised me by coming out to support the cause, which they had coordinated with my sister, Shannon. I very much appreciated their presence, as it was an emotional day. Additionally, I felt like they were making an effort to enter my special-needs world, which was touching. I can't say enough how extraordinary *all* my friends have been while I have stumbled down this less traveled road.

As a family, we spent a lot of our time at home. At home, we could make things more predictable for Liam, and therefore, it felt more manageable for us. Liam can be affectionate with both Bill and me; it just has to be on his terms and when he's open to it. I know we are both so grateful we get this unexpected gift from a son with Asperger's syndrome, as we know it is not the norm.

The smiles in this photo are about as authentic as it gets! Mira and I had just arrived at the neuropsychiatric temporary residential facility Liam was staying at in Texas. We were all so excited to be together! I remember it like it was yesterday, and I can't even put into words what it's like to be brought back to this moment. The anticipation of seeing Liam was heart pounding. I never knew exactly what his emotional and physical state would be like when I arrived, so to see his smiling face was spectacular.

This handsome, happy picture of Liam was taken at a subway stop in New York City. Ironically, we were in New York to see nationally renowned psychiatrist Dr. Demitri Papolos, who wrote *The Bipolar Child*. Although we had been told by two physicians in Michigan that Liam likely had early onset bipolar disorder, we sought Dr. Papolos's expertise to definitively diagnose him. This trip was yet another beginning as we were faced with the fact that Liam did indeed match the symptoms of the heartbreaking disorder. My uncle Dick always says knowledge is power. We certainly left New York with a lot more knowledge; we just needed to work on the power portion!

"Pick your battles" should be tattooed on the palms of all parents when they bring their children home! The Superman costume was not a battle I considered worth fighting. Liam wore some version of a Superman costume for over a year, and when I see pictures of him this way, I can't help but smile. In this photo he is golfing in Florida with my mom, at her country club. I love that she proudly marched in there with him, Superman costume and all!

If I added up the amount of money spent on Legos since Liam's birth, I am sure it would be astonishing. What I do know is that Liam is usually at his most content when he is constructing with Legos. I cherish the time we have spent over the years on the floor building together. I tried enrolling him in Lego camp and taking him to Lego KidsFest, both monumental flops. However, those hours at home, helping him find the perfect piece or watching him proudly show off a new creation are absolutely priceless!

All of my cookie sheets have somehow become Lego building platforms. I recently saw a quote on Pinterest that said, "There are three levels of pain: pain, excruciating pain, and stepping on a Lego." I laughed and winced at the same time, full well knowing what the unknown author was getting at. In this picture Liam is helping Mira complete one of her Lego sets. Let me make it very clear he would not be smiling if she were trying to "help" him build one of his. Sharing is definitely not one of Liam's strong suits!

Very early on Liam was fascinated with vacuums. If I were to take out the vacuum in front of Liam, I had to accept the fact that it wouldn't be possible to put it back in the closet until he was asleep. He was equally mesmerized by blow-dryers, and he dragged my unplugged dryer around the house on a regular basis. In this photo Liam had received a play vacuum as a gift. He was not very impressed and went straight for the closet!

There aren't many therapies we haven't tried with Liam over the years. I have to say therapeutic riding was definitely my favorite. I found a program where they allowed neurotypical siblings to ride as well, which was a huge selling point. Mira has spent countless hours in waiting rooms with me, as I try to entertain her with my bag full of tricks. Ultimately, she took to the horses much more than Liam, and for once, she didn't have to be the spectator.

Oh, how they have all grown! This picture is classic, with all the babies lined up for their monthly photo shoot. The time spent with all of our children together, lifelong friends giving support and encouragement to one another, was priceless. The mothers in our playgroup were all so authentic; there was absolutely no keeping up with the Joneses going on there! Liam is the third from the right. At the time he was only seven months old, and I had no clue what was ahead of us. His inability to sleep and sensitivity to sound were the only signs there was something a bit different about my sweet, little angel. It makes me both happy and sad to think back and remember what it was like before we knew what the future would hold.

Making the best of inpatient psychiatric facilities has kind of become our forte. This is my sister, Shannon, playing a game with Mira and Liam in the dayroom during his stay at a Chicago hospital. I spent the twenty-three nights at the Ronald McDonald House just a few blocks away. Liam was surprisingly peaceful while he was in the hospital, and I quickly got used to my three daily visits up to the pediatric psychiatric unit. When Mira stayed with me at the Ronald McDonald House and Liam was just around the corner, I oddly felt as if this could become a comfortable way to live. Liam was safe and being treated, Mira was safe and not across the country, and I had made friends at the house who almost felt like family. The boiling-frog theory strikes again!

"Occupational therapist" is another title I think I should hold, as a result of being Liam's mom. Our home has a "sensory chill zone," a place intended to help Liam decompress. I have spent hundreds of hours trying to help Liam's sensory system regulate. I have done sensory therapy in restaurants, at airports, and even at the beach. In this photo Liam is taking a sensory break at school, an attempt to organize his central nervous system so that he can participate more at school.

I can literally feel the joy I had in my heart at the time this photo was taken. The date was November 29, 2013, and I know this because it was the first time in eleven weeks that I had both of my children in my home! Liam had flown back from Texas that evening, and having them *both* in my arms, knowing they would both lay their heads on pillows in their own beds was indescribable. It felt like Christmas morning when I was a child! I was overcome with anticipation, excitement, and pure joy! Until this day, I believe having Liam admitted to that facility across the country was the hardest yet best decision I have ever made for our family. Even better than that, Liam finally views it the exact same way, even though sometimes he doesn't like to admit it.

Writing this book, sharing our journey, has been a labor of love. In some ways it has been difficult to share our most intimate truths, but in a lot of ways it has been cathartic. I have had the opportunity to see our reality for exactly what it is; good, bad and otherwise. When I needed to select an author photo, I knew immediately I wanted both Liam and Mira in the picture. I initially tried having professional pictures taken, to exude that "professional author" persona, but I quickly concluded that just wasn't our truth. This picture is our truth. Mira looks beautiful and happy, with her hair down and in a comfy T-shirt. Liam is looking away from the camera, which is always most comfortable for him, a classic characteristic of autistic people. As for me, I have on no makeup, sunglasses holding my hair back, and my two favorite accessories by my side! A girlfriend happened to snap the picture during the last day of school, a happy memory for all of us. This is more representative of our truth than any staged picture could ever be, and I love it!

Chapter 12

If You're Lucky, Life Is Humbling!

There are things you will find yourself doing in life that you *swore* you would never do. Nonetheless, you hear your mother's words coming out of your very own mouth, or you let a child sleep in your room because you are just too tired for the middle-of-the-night fight. These are the oh-so-humbling moments when you find yourself eating your words. If you have a sense of humor about it, you just chuckle and recognize how life teaches us lessons all day long.

Liam was the first grandchild on both sides of the family. Our parents and siblings had all kinds of opinions about how we were parenting our firstborn. I, like many exhausted first-time mothers, wished that every single challenge I was experiencing would be visited upon our sisters and brother when they became parents too. I couldn't wait for them to have a large serving of humble pie; it would be such justice!

Ironically, my sister had twins at forty-three years of age, and I find her random phone calls humbly admitting that she finally "gets it" so endearing. I no longer have that bitter resentment of wanting her to suffer, because I know now that if you are lucky, life is humbling. I smile when she explains how she now sees how hard it is to just get out of the house, not because I am glad she is struggling but because I am so glad she is part of the parenthood club.

Now, sometimes these humbling moments are small, like when you are at a restaurant with your whiny child and you remember back to a time of being single and finding that behavior soooo annoying! My child will never behave in that way, you'd smugly think to yourself in those days before humility. Those are small life lessons that gently shape us into better human beings. However, sometimes the humbling moments are life changing. They make you reevaluate what you ever thought or believed. They are poignant and profound, and they change you forever.

One profound reality check for me occurred when Liam was almost eight. Two clinicians recommended that Liam be medicated for his extreme anxiety. I remember that twenty-four-hour period like it was last week, and I remember thinking, thank you very much for your opinions. Have a nice day. I simply wasn't going to be one of *those* parents. In my naïve mind, I had preconceived notions about why parents used medications for neurobehavioral issues. I made assumptions, which I was ironically allowing to influence my parenting.

An even more life-changing moment occurred three years later, when, against everything I ever said, I decided having Liam admitted into a temporary residential program to treat his neuropsychiatric deficits was the only option left. It was an out-of-state facility I had diligently researched. I couldn't come to this excruciating conclusion without visiting the facility first, so my mom and I flew out there to meet the staff and learn as much as we possibly could.

Liam would literally be across the country from our home. I would have to leave him to the care of others for several months—a thought that I couldn't even conceptualize. Once he was there, I was able to visit my eleven-year-old child for long weekends only, and even then that time was limited, as the therapy he was receiving there couldn't constantly be interrupted by visitors. I wasn't able to tuck him into bed at night or fix him breakfast in the morning. This choice was unfathomable to me even just a few months before he went there, but then there I was, doing something I swore I would never do.

I remember distinctly when I heard about the temporary residential program available for kiddos just like Liam. I had learned of it years before. When I first heard about it, it was a place, in my mind, where parents took their children when they no longer wanted to be a part of the solution.

They were casting them off, and I thought those parents were monsters. I certainly had made some pretty brutal conclusions about family dynamics I had zero knowledge about.

It took me years to get to the decision to send Liam there. I promised myself I would *never* need to place Liam in such a facility. So how did he end up there when I'd promised myself I would never do so? It's called reality. Sometimes reality is so difficult to accept that it makes you feel like you can't breathe. When you do, you make choices that you never thought you would even consider!

Wow. That's all I can say about the ignorance and judgment I harbored in those early years of my journey. I had knee-jerk reactions regarding some things I knew very little about. I am now willing to say that fear and denial were probably the emotions I was masking with my judgment. I couldn't go down those terrifying roads. I simply wasn't ready to accept where things truly were at with Liam's struggles.

When we say things like "I'll never," we are setting ourselves up for failure. We are declaring how we will react to a situation before we have all the knowledge and wisdom that life has to offer us. We judge those who have traveled a road we know absolutely nothing about. It puts the relationships we have with both ourselves and others at risk.

Who did I think I was making those kinds of judgments? I had no clue what kind of roads those parents had been down or what kind of information they'd used to make their decisions. I didn't have the first idea what it was like to love a child so desperately that you were willing to do the unthinkable to give him or her a fighting chance.

To date, having Liam admitted to that amazing facility was the hardest yet bravest thing I have ever done. I had to dig deep down into the depths of my soul to muster up the strength to eat my own words. I had to admit to myself that any concept of control I had over Liam's struggles was an illusion. I had to be humble and venture onto a path I'd never wanted to explore. I feel brave because I had the strength to make this change, especially because I so desperately didn't want to.

Some people consider being humble a negative trait. I believe it is a gift. To be humble simply means showing that you do not think of yourself as better than other people. I believe having humility is the road to peace and gratitude. I know it took me time to find humility. I know I look back at that arrogant young woman I once was, and I chuckle at her. I know she wasn't intentionally judgmental or smug—she just hadn't received the gift of humility yet! I believe being Liam's mom has given me the opportunity to eat many servings of humble pie, and I am grateful for those lessons and the perspective this journey has provided.

Chapter 13

And Then There Were Two

Liam was already three and a half when we were blessed with the arrival of his beautiful sister, Mira. He had been dubbed "the Emperor" by my father, and it was a fitting title. It had been relatively easy to accommodate his "quirks" up to that point as he was all we had to focus on. Our entire family just ate him up and did a darn good job of convincing themselves, and trying to convince me, that Liam was absolutely, perfectly fine.

Although I knew Liam was quirky, I had no idea what was in store for Mira as she ventured through her journey as the sibling to a special-needs child. I have decided that "sibling of a special-needs child" could really be its very own diagnosis. So much comes along with those six extremely relevant words! Some of those things are gifts, but I would be remiss if I didn't say that many of them are struggles.

"She will learn to be so compassionate and accepting" is what I usually hear when I mention the difficulties Mira has in being Liam's sister. People also say how "strong and resilient" children are and that "she will be just fine." In response to these very supportive comments, I smile and agree. They are right. Remember what I said earlier: take what you like, and leave the rest. Mira *is* learning to be compassionate and accepting, and she is stronger and more resilient than any child I know. But to pretend this is the entire story would be selling her short. There is so much more than that to Mira's parallel journey next to Liam's life.

In some ways I think the birth order is relevant. For me, Liam's delays were all I'd ever known as a first-time parent. Although I am a pediatric nurse and I know the milestones like the back of my hand, I somehow normalized Liam's developmental progress. So as Mira progressed at an average pace, I was convinced she was gifted! I think most parents at some point believe their child is advanced in some way or another, but the contrast between a neurotypical and atypical child is so profound.

I imagine that if the firstborn were neurotypical but the second child atypical, the huge contrast would be painstaking; waiting for the next child to progress would be gut-wrenching. Either way, the discrepancies are brought to light and unavoidable. Siblings are compared in an average home, but the contrast when one child is impaired is so glaringly evident.

One of my best friends first had a daughter who was very bright. Less than two years later, she had a son who was on his own path, as all children are. Both of her children were neurotypical, but she would tell me how she found herself staring at her son, wondering if something was wrong. I still laugh at the story of how she and her husband would stand behind their son and clap to see if he'd flinch. They had convinced themselves he must be hearing impaired since he spent much of his time "on his own planet." That scenario is multiplied by a thousand when you live with the contrasts of an atypical and a neurotypical child all day long.

The birth-order thing also gets out of whack in a lot of ways. Sure, Liam is the big brother, but often Mira is forced to take on the role of big sister. It's usually not in the fun way either. It's not like she gets the benefits of being the older sibling, like getting a handheld gaming device first. It's more like she gets the rip-off portions of being the older sibling.

For example, I expect her to clean her room before she can go outside to play. When I find her clothes shoved onto the floor of her closet, I'll call her back in to properly straighten her room. With Liam, because he has such limited executive functions, I stay with him the entire time, coaching him through each and every step. She's eight, and he's twelve. I expect more of her because she can do more, but that doesn't mean it doesn't feel like a huge rip-off to Mira.

Oh sure, I've explained it to her every way I know how that she is capable of more, so if I lowered the bar for her, I'd being doing her a disservice. I sometimes even point out how grateful she should be that she has these capabilities. I bet I sound like Charlie Brown's teacher to Mira when I give her that spiel. I know in some ways she gets it, but it's also got to get old. She is way too smart to not pick up on the constant difference in expectations.

I ask more of Mira. I ask for her help when I am floundering, and I ask her to be on her own way more than she should have to be. When Liam is really struggling, and it's just the three of us, she's all I've got. Wow, does that sound like an incredible amount of pressure on my sweet eight-year-old, but it's the truth. Sure, it's all she's ever known, but that doesn't make it right. It's just the fact of the matter. She is able, and because of that, I expect more.

At the same time, it's confusing for me as a parent to identify what's "normal" anymore. I know people joke that normal is really just a setting on the washing machine, but there are some basic concepts of normal regarding what an average eight-year-old *should* be able to handle. Still, I get all mucked up because I live in alphabet-soup world, and my baseline is all kinds of screwed up. I find myself making accommodations for Liam and then feeling guilty that he gets off easier than Mira. Then I let things slide a bit with her, so that she doesn't feel such a profound contrast, but that's not right either. As you can imagine, there are constantly several conversations going on inside my head, trying to figure out which child's capabilities should be the driving force at any given time.

I find myself thinking so much about everything that I truly get sick of thinking. I want both of them to become their very best selves, but I can't get them there on the same train. They live in the same house, with the same mother, but their journeys are poles apart. Because of this difference, I have to approach them in different ways. I don't want to overaccommodate Mira and make her helpless, but I also don't want to put too much of the burden on this small person who is still so early in her own adventure. Needless to say, I spend a lot of my time reevaluating my parenting with both of them.

What I have come up with is this: if you have one special-needs child, then you have two. Mira inherently has special needs because she has a brother with special needs. I can't ignore the fact that being Liam's sister impacts her just like being Liam's mother impacts me. It is happening to her too.

I know that for Mira there have been gifts in being Liam's sister. She has learned that we all have gifts and we all have struggles. She hears me remind them both of this all the time. She has learned that what's fair for one isn't always the same for the other. This is a priceless life lesson from which we all can benefit. Mira has learned to advocate for herself, which is something I desperately want for both of my children. She has learned to forgive in a way that I envy. In fact, I told Liam recently that she loves him unconditionally, and that is a gift he will very rarely receive.

I look at Mira, and I am in awe. She is spunky, smart, funny, sensitive, independent, and beautiful. She has not only taught me how to be a better mother but also how to be a better person. She looks at Liam from a perspective that only she can. She accepts him completely because, from the moment she came into this world, her concept of "brother" was simply "Liam."

Chapter 14

Thank God for Grandparents! I Think I'm Going to Choke Them!

This chapter, much like all of them, has been a work in progress from the moment I became a mother. I think the relationship between parents and their child's grandparents is a fragile work of art. I would venture to guess that the grandparents would agree about the fragile part. The relationship is so vulnerable yet critical at the same time. That is a lot of pressure on all the people involved.

The one thing I want to make crystal clear is that I feel blessed every single day for the grandparents my children have. I know they all have done the very best they can with what has been a very challenging set of circumstances. As I mentioned, it took me a long time to realize this was happening to them too. We were all having our very own experience, and so much was to be learned by each of us. The growth that has occurred within the circle of our family has been extraordinary. I could not be more thankful for the progress we have *all* made.

That being said, it hasn't always been a pretty road. I think it's important to express the things I've learned about grandparents and myself and about how these relationships have so much potential if we nurture them and give them the benefit of the doubt. I hope these thoughts help you strengthen your irreplaceable relationships.

1.   *Grandparents have been waiting to be grandparents for a very long time!*

What this means is they have built up expectations and ideas in their heads that you have absolutely no clue about. They have taken bits of their own history, their friends' stories, and information from the media to come up with a scenario that they are incredibly excited to experience. Every day that you are anticipating the arrival of your baby, the grandparents are anticipating the arrival of their baby's baby! Their baby is having a baby; what an emotional experience for them! They are proud, excited, and nervous. They are experiencing yet another one of the rites of passage and have a ton of unknowns just over the horizon.

2.   *The role of grandparents is a dependent one; they can't become grandparents unless someone else supplies the baby.*

This is an uncomfortable spot for the matriarchs and patriarchs of our families. For a very long time, our parents have been in the driver's seat. They have gotten to head things up, be the advice givers, and show the way. But the role of grandparent is a tricky one. Their baby now has a baby. Although they have all kinds of ideas about how you should go about dressing, bathing, and feeding the new family member, they simply aren't in charge. This is *your* child, and most of us are very territorial of our newborn babies. Our mama or papa bear instincts come out, and even our own parents' words of wisdom aren't more powerful than our instincts.

This leaves our parents in a very unfamiliar role. They don't know where they fit but desperately want to be a part of this new chapter. We need to keep in mind that they are in unchartered territory and are trying to get their footing, just as we are as new parents. It would behoove all of us to embrace one another and find humor in the stumbling that is bound to occur.

You will get very sick of hearing, "Well, when you were a baby..." The most annoying thing my mom would continually mention was that there weren't so many rules when I was little. "It's amazing you survived back in the day!" she'd say sarcastically. How that would chap my ass! But it always went better when I'd take a second to explain why a rule existed, instead of acting as if she were clueless. I'm sure there was a very good reason why our mothers added rice cereal to our bottles and then cut the nipple a bit so that we could suck it down. They weren't idiots, and neither are we; we are just dealing with a whole new set of information and research that their generation didn't have. Cut them some slack, and chances are they will cut you some as well.

3. *Although it is hard to comprehend, your parents love you just as much as you love your child.*

I referenced this earlier, and I think it's crucial that we revisit this truth. You've heard your parents say for years, "You'll understand when you're a parent." However, you can't understand until it happens. I think the love we have for our own children is so incredibly personal and profound that we find it hard to believe anyone ever loved or loves us like that. So I think the more fitting comment would be, "You'll finally understand when you're a grandparent."

Maybe that's when we'll finally get to come full circle and comprehend what kind of love our parents felt for us all those years during the many phases of our lives. The grandparents are the generation of our family who have had the opportunity to love their children as babies, kids, adults, and finally as parents to their very own children, our parents' grandchildren. Their love for us never ceases, just as our love will never cease for our own children. So many things are backward in life, and this is just another one of those things we don't grasp until far after it's helpful. That sucks for all of us, our parents included, because we don't appreciate their perspective until it's no longer advantageous.

4. *The fact that your child has special needs is hitting the grandparents as a double whammy!*

A surefire way to rile me up is to tell me you know how challenging it is to be a parent to a child with special needs (unless you have one too, and then we can compare war stories). This comment, depending on my mood, may set me into a bit of a huff. The grandparents have told me they hurt about, think about, worry about, or care about Liam's circumstances just as much as me. Now, I can move forward with this one of two ways. I can realize that they truly believe this and just want me to know that I am not in the trenches alone, or I can turn it into a pissing contest. I am not proud to say that for a long time I went the contest route, and it never turned out pretty.

What I have come to realize is that grandparents have a double dose of every emotion they experience regarding the reality of having a grandchild with special needs. Remember those expectations I talked about earlier? I am pretty sure their expectations looked a lot more like them taking their grandson fishing than taking him to occupational therapy. I am confident that almost all grandparents anticipated afternoons of picnics in the park with their baby and their baby's baby. They couldn't wait to share in your joy. It was going to be magical! And then...

All of a sudden, nothing looks like they thought it would. Sure, it doesn't look like we, the parents, thought it was going to either, but our parents are experiencing the mourning process times two—once as grandparents of a special-needs grandchild and once as parents to their child who is dealing with raising a special-needs child. Yes, they are devastated that their journeys as grandparents are going to look different from what they expected. At the same time, just as we see all the hopes and dreams for our children being altered, they are seeing their hopes and dreams for their children to marry, have children, and live happily ever after being altered too.

Our parents want us to have lives free of suffering and pain. They don't want to see us struggle. They want to make it better, but they simply can't. Our reality has changed their reality, and they can't do a damn thing about it. Wow! Think about how gut-wrenching that must be for them. They are watching their grandchild go down the road less traveled, and we are right beside that grandchild holding his or her hand. Our folks are watching two of the most precious people on the planet to them go down a difficult road. Just as we have had to change our hopes and dreams for our child, our parents are changing their hopes and dreams for their child *and* grandchild. They have to do it twice, so it is more than painful for them.

5.   *When grandparents offer suggestions or advice, they are doing the best they know how to support both us and our child.*

My suggestion here is to go back and reread chapter 6, "When We Know Better, We Do Better," and chapter 7, "I

Wish There Was More I Could Do to Help!" All of the ideas in these chapters completely pertain to our parents as well. They are doing the best they can with what they've got.

Most likely they are just trying to share a bit of their knowledge, history, or traditions with the next generation. They are not intending to offend you or take over your life. Well, maybe they are trying to take over a little bit, but it's because being the older and wiser family member is all they've known. Their role has often been to guide and support us; they're not used to watching *us* do the guiding and supporting. This is a whole new ball game for our parents, and they are slowly learning the rules.

There is an old saying, "The shortest distance between two people is a smile." I think this is the first step toward bridging the gap between generations. Smile—a lot. Smile because you are finally a parent. Smile because you get to share in this experience with people who love you as much as you love your child. Smile because, during your very best and very worst parenting moments, there are people who want to share the joys and the burdens. Most importantly, remember the grandparents are hurting as well, times two! Cut them some slack, and hug them. A hug often improves the worst of situations, and as you all embark on the road less traveled, you all could probably use one, or even two!

Chapter 15

Where Are All the Casserole Dishes?

I make the same meal for all of my friends whenever they have a baby or, conversely, have a death in the family. It's my go-to move, and I've heard it's quite good. If you have a family member added or deleted, you get my cheesy mostaccioli casserole, garlic bread, a salad, and Ghirardelli triple-chocolate brownies. This is what I do. Additionally, if you have an otherwise difficult situation going on in your life, I may go this route as well. When a close friend's husband broke his hip and was wheelchair bound for some time—casserole. A friend was taking care of her mother a lot when her mom was going through chemo—casserole. A friend had back surgery—casserole.

So I assume you're getting the theme here: when people are in chaos, I feel compelled to help in some way, and a common way to do that in our culture is to make them food. In many ways I think the casserole dishes are symbolic. It's more about acknowledging that a person is going through a significant period in his or her life and you think enough of that person to want to lighten the load.

That being said, I would like to mention that the chaos that ensues in the household of a child with special needs would warrant a casserole delivered multiple times a week. There are days when I truly believe one for breakfast and another at dinnertime would not be overdoing it. If there was a mathematical formula that qualified people for casserole delivery, I am confident special-needs families would come out as the correct answer much of the time.

Truthfully, however, we are usually left thinking, where are *our* casserole dishes? Now, most of us wouldn't say this out loud, but I bet if you asked, one zebra to another, if anyone has had this thought, most of us would admit we have. Heck, even Liam got teary the other day and asked, "Mom, why are there always so many sad commercials about kids with cancer, but no one wants to help kids like me?" Of course, I took that opportunity to teach him all about National Autism Awareness Month and how buildings all over the world "Light It Up Blue." I also told him there is a

Mental Health Awareness Month, but even I, a person who is very involved in all things mental health, had to look it up to tell him when it was. The fact of the matter is that we have made enormous strides as a culture in the realm of special needs, but, wow, do we have a long way to go!

I think there are at least two different reasons why families of special-needs children don't make the casserole cut. First of all, our day-to-day chaos has sort of become our norm and, therefore, the norm others have accepted for our lives. It's that whole boiling-frog theory. We have adapted to our chaos, and, therefore, the people who care about us have adapted to our chaos as well. I would imagine it's pretty similar to an adult who's been suffering with multiple sclerosis or Crohn's disease. It's not that people don't care; they just get desensitized to our daily plight.

Secondly, I think it's awkward for people to determine when things have gotten bad enough for them to show up with a casserole. If it was difficult for me as Liam's mother to determine if he was struggling enough to have him evaluated, how do we expect other people to know when we are *really* sinking in the quicksand? I bet people are hesitant to essentially say with their symbolic casserole, "Wow, it looks like your life sucks so bad right now that I thought I should bring you a casserole."

So, I am again going to refer to chapter 7, "I Wish There Was More I Could Do to Help." When people ask what they can do, for heaven's sake, give them an honest answer. If you know next week your child has three different therapy appointments, an MRI, and your husband is going to be out of town, when your girlfriend asks if there is anything she can do, say yes! Say a meal would be wonderful!

At one point Liam was hospitalized in Chicago for twenty-three days. This was an out-of-state hospital stay for our family, and I remained in Chicago the entire time, staying at the Ronald McDonald House. I can't say enough about the amazing experience I had while staying there. If you ever get a moment, look into all that the McDonald's charity offers to families in crisis.

One thing I profoundly remember was how much the generously prepared meals, provided by the house and its volunteers, made a difference. I desperately needed a warm meal to fill my empty soul at the end of my long days. The lunchtime meal was perfect for breaking up the monotony of traveling back and forth to the hospital, and it somehow provided some sense of normality.

When I returned from this long adventure, my girlfriend Heather asked if I minded if she set up a service called Meal Train. It was an online organizer that facilitated my friends signing up for days to bring me a meal. Initially I thought the storm was over once I was home, and I diminished the need for such help. Heather, having a special-needs son herself, knew better and really encouraged me to accept the support of my friends. It was wonderful! My friends felt like they could then really support me, since they couldn't do much while I was away, and the meals took a big load off my plate as I got reestablished with Mira and Liam back home.

Food is something that connects us all. When others prepare it for you, it allows them to share a piece of themselves. It gives us a reason to stop, sit down, and rejoice in that brief time we have together. In the words of Virginia Woolf, "One cannot think well, love well, and sleep well, if one has not dined well."

Chapter 16

Living in the Moment While Waiting for the Other Shoe to Drop

This is the very unorthodox way I spend most of my days. I am not going to say this is a tranquil way to exist, but it's kind of the way I've learned to function inside the confines of our reality. I've learned that if I am not able to do both simultaneously—live in the moment and wait for the other shoe to drop—I am not able to fluidly bounce back from the expected "unexpected moments" in our day-to-day lives.

The following story is a perfect example of this skill. I recently had a last-minute opportunity to grab lunch with a friend. If I were inflexible, I wouldn't have been able to jump at the chance, since, heaven knows, planning ahead doesn't work out so well for me most of the time—Liam's unpredictability makes sure of that! I had a few things on my agenda, but all of them were pretty low priority, so I took him up on the lunch date. I was ready to head out the door when Liam's school called to let me know he wasn't doing well and they needed for me to come in. Bam! I had to grab a protein bar in the car on the way to school and tell my friend I'd catch up with him later. The date was rescheduled for dinner, as the kids were spending the night with their dad. Simple enough! But when it was time for drop-off at their father's, Liam was unable to transition. Bottom line, he was having a low-functioning day, and no matter how excited I was for my dinner plans, they just weren't going to happen.

I am grateful that I was born with a pretty easygoing personality. I love my sister to death, but with her type-A personality, I am confident she would be losing her mind with this kind of unpredictability. My sis is always so sweet about telling me it is no coincidence I am Liam's mom. Certainly, my ability to go with the flow is a needed match for his inability to do the same.

I have found that if I have baseline expectations and take the rest as the icing on the cake, then I am not walking around feeling mopey all the time. Most of the time things don't go how we expect them to go anyhow. So if we just have minimal expectations, when the other shoe does drop, we do a pretty good job of catching it midair.

Parenting Liam has taught me that very few things are as crucial as we initially thought they were. All of our lists and priorities aren't really as important as seizing the moment when a good one comes along. Liam's inflexibility has given me a crash course in needing to be extremely flexible. I have found this is a gift in all aspects of life, personally and professionally. It makes me a better mom, sister, and friend. I don't get bent out of shape the way I used to, and I am grateful for that!

I have also learned that often the rat race is exactly what destabilizes all of us. If I just slow the heck down, our whole house functions a ton better, and we don't let real moments fly by. I have learned to take the time to smell the roses, as they say. When Liam is having a high-functioning evening, I relish in it. The laundry and dishes will certainly still be there later, but his positive, functional mood may not be!

This way of going about life has brought me so many unexpected, joyous memories. There have often been times when I was planning for one experience but have been led to an even better experience. My sister always says, "Option A didn't work. Pick again!" I love that she taught me that. We can always pick again!

So, fifth-grade camp was way too much stimulation for Liam; pick again! I did, so we left and went out to lunch, just the two of us, and had a wonderful afternoon. Liam was having a very low-functioning day at school, and they thought it would be best for me to pick him up. I picked again, and we went to an exotic-bird rescue and made friends with a beautiful cockatoo name Prince, which we otherwise would never have known about.

Picking again is a life lesson. It can be applied to plans, relationships, and careers, really anything! It all depends on our ability to consider our options while living in the moment. I have taught my kids the same mantra my father taught me: there are always options! I will say to my children, "Guys, there's always a what?" and they'll chime in, "Solution." Solutions are come to by considering your options. At the end of the day, life comes down to whether you are going to catch the shoe and run with it or let it hit you in the head and knock you down. Never forget: there's always a solution!

Chapter 17

Nothing Ever Turns Out Quite How We Imagined

I can't begin to tell you how unpredictable life can be when participating in social or public situations with a child with special needs. There are so many dynamics going on all at once; it actually makes my head spin to even write about it. Walking in is only a sliver of the scenario! So much has happened leading up to and getting to the event, and Lord knows, a ton can transpire once, or if, we finally make it there!

I often get anxiety about planning things with Liam. I realize I just wrote a chapter about how I have learned to embrace the unexpected, but bringing Liam out into the social realm of the world is still something I have not mastered a Zen feeling about. You see, there are a thousand things that play into what a social outing will look like with Liam. For starters, just because I think an activity will be a great match, doesn't mean it is. It never ceases to amaze me how very wrong I can be!

A perfect example was my brilliant idea of taking Liam to Lego KidsFest. Two years ago, I found out Lego was launching an expo for all things Lego. Liam has been obsessed with Legos from the moment he first saw them. We literally have bins and bins of Legos, and I use three-ring binders to house all of the instruction manuals for every set we've ever owned. He has a Lego alarm clock. I built shelves to display all of his Lego creations. I couldn't think of something more up Liam's alley than a Legofest!

I got tickets the moment they became available, and I coordinated with my family for them to come as well. My sister was bringing her stepson, who is one of Liam's very favorite people. I was so excited about this perfect day; it would be nothing short of ideal for my little buddy! We walked in, and ten minutes later Liam walked out. He didn't see the amazing life-size Batman or R2-D2 or the Lego Masters building spectacular creations. He didn't care that there was a free play area where he could have endless access to every single Lego imaginable. Liam didn't join in with all the children who were overjoyed to be there. He didn't see how excited I was to watch him be part of this amazing day—a day I thought was his perfect scenario.

From Liam's perspective, all he saw was too many people, too many colors, too big a building, and too bright lights. There were too many smells from the concession stand and too much noise from the people announcing all the upcoming activities and competitions. Now, I am not totally clueless. Once he pointed out all of these very obvious triggers, I had an aha moment, but leading up to it, I was just sure I had nailed it!

These moments, when you have put your whole heart into planning the perfect day for your child only to have it all go wrong, are nothing short of depressing. My lifelong friend Andrea and I call these moments "prom." What we mean by this is that some moments can never be what we have built them up to be in our heads. The high-school prom was like that for both of us and, I imagine, for a lot of people. Remember all the preparation that went into your prom? You searched for the perfect dress and the perfect shoes, and you made sure your date's cummerbund matched just so. You coordinated with your friends so you could all go together and then...

Life doesn't always turn out the way we planned it in our heads. Often it's because of things entirely out of our control, such as your date ending up getting food poisoning or the limo breaking down. Sometimes, though, we romanticize how we think things *should* turn out, and it's rare for real life to live up to such expectations. Expectations can lead us down a road of disappointment. Unrealistic expectations most certainly will do so!

What I have learned thus far is to evaluate my expectations and find a balance between over- and underthinking things when it comes to making plans for Liam. I don't want to overthink things, or we'll never leave the house. But if I don't put some realistic thought into whether or not a scenario is appropriate for my little angel, then I am setting us up for failure. Liam loves monster trucks, but after very little thought I know, without a shadow of a doubt, a monster-truck rally would be living hell for my guy.

Another thing I've come to accept is that we can always give something a try, and if it doesn't work out, then we can simply leave. This way does make it a bit inconvenient when planning things, because then I need to drive separately so as to not disrupt other's plans. Still, the extra car is more than worth it if a meltdown occurs and we need a quick getaway. I have also found that bringing an extra adult is never a bad idea, because I have two kids, and that way Mira isn't constantly forced to live inside Liam's restricted world.

Tweaking an idea is just the ticket sometimes too. For example, I really wanted to take my kids for an overnight adventure. I had heard many friends talking about what a great time they had with their kids at an indoor water park. After a failed attempt at doing this over spring break last year, I realized that for Liam less is more. The lines were more than he could handle, and the huge facility was way too overwhelming for him. Next time I want to do a water getaway with Liam, I will find a neat hotel that has a fun indoor pool along with a game room. Liam will have much more fun in this scaled-down environment, and I will too! It's a great lesson for all of us that we don't always need the bells and whistles to have a wonderful time.

I continue to grow and learn about ways to make all of us more comfortable with integrating into society. I have to constantly juggle between underthinking, overthinking, and thinking outside the box, but it is more than worth it. I will always strive to integrate Liam into the neurotypical world, doing so in ways that will allow him to feel safe, secure, and proud to be exactly who he is!

Chapter 18

To Med or Not to Med, That Is the Question!

There are so many times we as parents must make momentous decisions during the course of our children's lives: How long do I breastfeed? Day care or home with my sister-in-law? Fruits or veggies first? To circumcise or not to circumcise? Each one of these decisions seems to have so much weight at the time. It feels as though if we choose the wrong answer, we may flat-out ruin our children.

One of these major decisions is about medication for our special-needs child. What can I say about the mass numbers of conflicting opinions? One study will show, without a shadow of a doubt, how you should handle something, while an equally substantiated study will show the polar opposite result. Now throw in the grandparents' opinions, which may vary considerably, and you've got a reason for pulling your hair out. Sometimes being the one to make the final decision is a burden no one cares to bear.

One hypersensitive topic for a parent of a child with special needs is whether or not to medicate for neuro-behavioral symptoms. You may wonder why I specified this type of symptoms, and I can give you a pretty cut-and-dried answer. When your child has diabetes, there is a blood test given that is as concrete as it gets. It is crystal clear how much insulin that child requires to stay healthy and safe. I would venture to guess a huge number of parents whose children have neuro-behavioral disorders would sign up for a concrete test in a heartbeat! It would be such a gift to have something in writing that proves, without question, that giving your child a mood-altering medication is the sure way to go.

Instead, we are given the burden of ultimately making this decision based on the guidance of professionals, our own research, our preconceived notions about medications, and, ultimately, our gut. Then you have to have the strength and courage to defend this decision when often you don't even know if it was the right one to begin with.

I will never forget the day I was told Liam needed to be on medication for anxiety. I actually had two different clinicians at two separate appointments tell me the same exact thing, which was ironic because I hadn't asked either of them for an opinion. When Liam's occupational therapist told me she didn't think sensory therapy was alleviating Liam's anxiety and that she felt we were at a point where we needed to consider a medication to help him be more comfortable in his body, I said, thanks for your thoughts, and left. I wasn't mad, but I also completely ignored her opinion, because I wasn't at a place where I could hear her words.

Less than twenty-four hours later, Liam's psychologist told me he really believed we had given cognitive-behavioral therapy a fighting chance but that Liam appeared to have physiological anxiety, which needed to be medicated. I started laughing. This was probably not the reaction he was prepared for, and so he inquired why I was chuckling. I told him about the conversation I had had just one day prior with Liam's OT, and he asked if I had intended to mention that recommendation.

I candidly said I hadn't because, as far as I was concerned, we weren't "there" yet. "There" was a place I couldn't let myself go. It symbolized so many things I wasn't prepared to own. It meant I couldn't will away Liam's struggles. It meant that, soon enough, grandparents, aunts, and uncles would know we had gone down "that" road. It meant I was going to have to defend a decision for which I had no blood test to prove that I had done my due diligence and made the very best decision to keep Liam healthy and safe.

I remember standing in the vestibule at the doctor's office crying, calling Liam's father to tell him we were faced with another unchartered territory. I am pretty sure he cried too. How do you make a decision about something that isn't concrete? We knew Liam was suffering. We knew Liam's little body was being taxed by an invisible illness. We knew that we had to do something because to do nothing would be inhumane.

Thankfully, Liam's father and I agreed about the decision. We decided to give it a try. We knew that what we were doing wasn't working and that we had exhausted all other options. We were a united front with this decision, and I am so grateful for that. Sometimes it's just a matter of taking all that you know for certain and then taking a leap of faith.

Since that first medication, Liam has been on and off so many different meds. I have struggled with each change and poured over research to help me feel at peace with each decision. We have tried medications knowing the side effects were scary as hell but knowing, at the same time, Liam's symptoms were even scarier. I have gone through periods where I felt as though none of it made a lick of difference, and I've gone through stretches full well knowing medications have given my son a fighting chance.

People will judge your decisions all of your life. Sometimes they will tell you outright, and other times they'll judge you from afar. I've learned a poignant concept, and I think it applies here: what others think of you is really none of your business. Kind of an odd way to look at it, but at the end of the day, your business is to consider what you think of yourself.

Can you look yourself in the mirror and know you did everything you possibly could to keep your child healthy and safe? Did you review the data and consider the many options? Did you do your due diligence? Are you advocating for your child because that's a burden you are proud and honored to take on? I think if the answer to all of those things is yes, then no matter what decision you make, you are making the right one, and you are brave for making it!

Chapter 19

Dating When You Live in a Special-Needs World

I can honestly say there are times I look around and wonder what the #*@! happened to my life. I am forty-two; divorced with two kids, one of whom has special needs; and I have had a profile on Match.com! Seriously, this is my life. My stepmom jokes all the time that there should be a dating website for special-needs, single parents. I think she's got a pretty solid idea there, because getting a single parent of a neurotypical child to understand your special-needs world has proven to be pretty darn challenging!

My kids make it entertaining to say the least. Liam's autism makes it difficult for him to understand that this is actually happening to *me.* He only looks at it from the perspective of what's in it for him. He makes requests that completely crack me up! When Bill and I first split up, Liam informed me that he hoped his dad would get a "hot girlfriend." Fair enough, I thought, although he didn't need to mention it only two weeks post-separation. Liam then followed up with his hope that I would marry a girl, because he wanted a baby brother or sister, and he knew I couldn't have any more children. I thought to myself, seriously? Your dad gets a hot chick, and I'm becoming gay? It still cracks me up when I think about it! You have to love autism and its lack of perspective. Mira's requests often involve her interests, like wanting me to date someone who has a child that plays basketball or has a dog. It has not crossed either of their minds to consider what *I* might be looking for in a partner, but in time, maybe it will.

For me there was initially a ton of apprehension, because I knew it was going to take an amazing man to sign up for my gig, and there was fear I'd never find him. There are so many details to navigate in general when you are dating and have kids, but a special-needs kiddo adds a whole other dimension. When do you divulge the details? How much information do you share?

Obviously I can write a book about it, but you don't want to overwhelm someone too early on. On the other hand, you also don't want to wait too long, because if he or she isn't up for your reality, then that individual is *out*! As I always tell my kids, whomever Mommy finally picks for our family, he gets us as a package deal! Liam, being autistic and often hyperfocused on details, always adds that the man *must* love our two cats and his guinea pig as well!

I have two different theories about how to maneuver through this tricky new world. Which theory I use at any given moment often hinges on my mood and where things are with Liam's stability at the time. I don't think one is more right than wrong. I guess I just feel out my comfort level at the time and go from there.

The first one is low and slow. This is the approach many of Liam's doctors have taken when beginning a new medication, and I like it. I don't wait too long to mention Liam has some special needs, but I offer a low number of details. As things slowly move along, I give more information and assess whether I think this person is generally interested in hearing our story. I am protective of our truths and share them only when I see the person becoming invested. I try to be gradual, but honestly, that's not my nature.

The second theory is ready, set, go! I don't completely inundate the person with every medical detail, but I am pretty upfront that my life is a bit atypical. I am kind of a what-you-see-is-what-you-get type of person, so this approach is probably what is most comfortable for me. I don't feel like I am hiding anything that way, and I am being true to my children, in particular Liam. If I'm honest, I think sometimes I do this ready-set-go approach to expedite the process. If you are going to be in my life, then you have to accept that Liam and Mira, for that matter, are special. My children are special in a zillion ways, but it's not going to be a typical journey if you take us on. That's kind of a take-it-or-leave-it approach. I have found there are some people who don't flinch and others who kindly back off immediately. Either way I am OK with the reaction; I'd just rather know it sooner than later!

I was recently talking to a friend who said something really hopeful. I was telling her how I was uncertain about finding a man who would fit into our puzzle. I was saying how it will be really hard to find someone who will wholeheartedly embrace our reality. She pointed out, so lovingly, how I should really look at that as a gift. She went on to say that maybe if I didn't have special circumstances, I wouldn't have my bar set so high for the man I let into our lives. She got me to see the silver lining! I will end up with an amazing man *because* of Liam's struggles. Whomever we accept into our lives, and who, in turn, accepts us into his life, will be an extraordinary man because he will have to be, and that makes me smile!

Chapter 20

You Really Need to Take Care of Yourself

For many years this advice was absolutely infuriating to me! I used to think, easy for you to say. Do you have any idea what my days look like? Are you kidding me? A manicure and pedicure are not going to change my reality one single iota! I felt as if people were minimizing my situation, insinuating that going for a walk or meeting friends for lunch would somehow change the drama of my life. How completely clueless of them, I'd think to myself.

Parenting, in general, is a pass-the-baton type of job. It's never done and wrapped up all pretty before we go to bed at night. There are the wake-up-in-the-middle-of-the-night moments. The smaller ones are when you realize something like your second grader failed to study for his or her weekly spelling test. The big moments occur when you can focus on absolutely nothing else, like when your son is driving alone for the very first time and you are waiting with baited breath for his arrival phone call. The laundry is never done, the house is never clean enough, and as parents, we are grossly aware of these facts.

For a special-needs parent, the worries are all encompassing. What we don't do for our child today could have long-term ramifications for his or her quality of life in the future. This is a staggering thought, and I'm going to say it again because it is what drives us and makes us incapable of taking care of ourselves. We fear that what we don't do for our child today could have long-term ramifications for his or her quality of life in the future. Wow, that is heavy! How do you go fishing with a buddy knowing that kind of responsibility is hanging over your head?

The amount of pressure we put on ourselves to make sure not one tiny stone is left unturned is astonishing. This pace is how I measured my success as a parent for a very long time. I couldn't cure Liam's special needs or make Mira's childhood typical, but damn it, I was going to die trying! I was going to be able to say at the end of my journey that there was nothing I didn't try to make sure the quality of life for both of my children reached its absolute, fullest potential! Sadly, what I didn't consider was that *my* quality of life was a huge indicator of how solidly I could advocate for my children's quality of life.

This mind-set lasted for a very long time. Part of it was that I felt extremely guilty for carving out any "me" time. I thought time not spent with the kids should be spent learning about and researching ways to better their lives. My mind never stopped, and honestly, I didn't have the first clue about how to shut it off, even if I wanted to. I was obsessed with improving Liam's and Mira's lives, and in the process, I was becoming a shell of myself, my identifying role being caregiver and mother.

Even when I did try to take care of myself, my reality was still in the forefront of my mind. I felt as if I were actually just faking it, pretending I was relaxing, and that really pissed me off. Why would I want to go to lunch with a bunch of friends who were talking about soccer camp or the honor roll when Liam had occupational therapy that evening or could barely read? It seemed as if this concept of taking time for myself was making me feel worse instead of better. I didn't walk away from those moments refreshed and peaceful. I usually ran back home feeling guilty and resentful.

What I do know for sure is that I was well intended. I truly felt I was doing right by my children by making them the primary focus of my life. I believed I'd be less of a mother, somehow betraying them, if I took time for myself. I reasoned that our struggles would still exist and would not be getting better if I was gallivanting about being happy and carefree. I simply refused to consider that using my time to decompress, relax, and recharge had any kind of value...and then my body told me I didn't have a choice.

My dad has always said, "Kid, you're the linchpin holding it all together. If you go down, it all goes down." Both my parents have always been greatly aware of how dedicated I am to my family. I have learned, though, that because I am their daughter, they are equally dedicated to me. They, along with my supportive family and friends, could see me slowly losing any sense of who I was. I barely recognized myself as I was beyond exhausted, angry, resentful, and sad.

To see me from the outside, you'd have thought I had it all together. I still smiled in the school office when I signed the kids in and out from school. I'd chat with you if I saw you at the grocery store. I still showered and picked up the house. I even managed to throw on mascara and lip gloss most days. However, inside I was crumbling, and it felt *awful*. All those years of being optimistic and energetic, often compared to Tigger from *Winnie-the-Pooh*, had finally caught up with me, and I no longer was the Little Engine That Could.

I remember the week my body shut down like it was yesterday, and the timing was quite interesting. It wasn't when Liam received diagnosis after diagnosis. It wasn't when I was flying back and forth between Michigan and Texas with my children on opposite sides of the country. It wasn't when the kids' dad and I split up. All those times, it would have made complete sense for me to curl up into a ball and stop functioning, yet I kept it together! I always managed to hyperperform during the most chaotic of times. And then—

It was a regular, old week, relative to our lives. Liam was doing pretty well, which meant he hadn't been restrained recently and could attend school. Mira was thriving and starting softball season, which she loved. My friends and family were all still by my side. It was a time I should have been soaking it all in, really feeling grateful for the reprieve. But that week I had a falling out with a close friend, and that was simply more than I could take!

At the time I kept thinking, what is my problem? Seriously, as if this is the most devastating thing I've ever been through! But it felt like my world was ending, and I was falling into a black hole. I vacillated between feeling despondent and irrational and feeling numb and completely cerebral. I felt completely batshit crazy and could feel myself unraveling. I hated how I felt and was at a complete loss as to how to recover.

I tried all my go-tos: calling my sis, going to the gym, doing my daily motivational readings, organizing the house, all to no avail. I started losing interest in everything; I didn't want to talk to people, didn't want to go anywhere, and really didn't even want to interact with my kids. I was scattered, disconnected, and completely out of steam. I couldn't stop crying and had thoughts I knew were abnormal.

The gratitude I have for the people in my life who have said, "If you ever need anything, *I am here*," is indescribable. I know there are many people who would have been there for me in an instant had they known how dark my mind had become. However, I reached out to only a few, and wow, did they deliver. Two women in particular could clearly see I wasn't myself, and I trusted them enough to share my truth.

As hard as it was to admit, I knew, and so did they, that I had reached some sort of threshold. My body could no longer run on caffeine, ice cream, and optimism. The brutal reality of my life and the lives of my sweet children had drained every ounce of oomph Tigger had. So I was left with a decision: give up or step up. For me, giving up would never be an option and stepping up would mean I needed to make some real changes, so I was once again at *another* beginning.

This meant reframing who I was. I was a mother who had two children, one with special needs, but I was, and am, a lot more than that. My children need to see that their mother is a person who has value and needs. They need to see me model a balanced life, and that means making myself a priority as well. I realized that week that if I was going to continue being an amazing mother, then I needed to take care of Kelly. If Kelly wasn't OK, then she couldn't be strong enough to persevere through what would certainly be one hell of a ride.

I hesitated to share what some of this reframing entailed, but I decided if I'm not completely honest, how can I expect you to trust me as a fellow zebra? For me, it looked like this: I accepted my reserves were tapped and I didn't have the ability to regroup with a simple trip to the spa. I needed help, like many people do, so I decided to see a doctor. My doctor and I decided going on medication was the best solution for *me* at that time. I say that with no shame, no regret, and a lot of resolve. I believe I was at the lowest point I had ever been, and I was nowhere near the finish line. I needed a multifaceted solution, and medication was part of that plan.

I also became more committed to me time, which meant doing things that made me more balanced. You see, up to this point I'd looked at me time as futile because the problems would still be there when the me time was over. Now I look at it from a different angle; I need the me time *because* the problems are still there when it's over and decompressing makes me much more capable of tackling our truth. I no longer feel guilty when I grab lunch with a girlfriend or go for a long walk in the park. I now know I am taking good care of Liam and Mira's mom, just like I would a dear friend, and she is more than worth it!

Chapter 21

The Gift Has Yet to Be Revealed

"The gift has yet to be revealed" is sometimes the hardest thing to believe, but once you truly do, it makes getting through even the most horrific of scenarios possible. With all my heart, I know that good comes from everything, and it is one of the only things I will promise you in this book. This belief doesn't in any way diminish how difficult life can be at times, but looking for the gift can sometimes be all it takes to turn our energy around. The promise of a gift can be the one thing that helps us start yet another beginning, get up from licking our wounds, and move from the past into the future.

Now this is entirely different from the old saying, "Somewhere, someone else has it way worse off than you." Although this saying is very true, it isn't exactly a positive spin on our already-difficult situation. When people say that, I always wonder, are they trying to make me feel guilty for feeling the way I do, or are they trying to make me more depressed by thinking of all the tragic situations out there? Recently someone told me you can be grateful and unhappy at the same time. Holy cats, did that make a whole lot of sense to me. It explains why I can be grateful that Liam isn't as sick as some children but still be heartbroken that he has so much to contend with.

Looking for the gifts, however, is searching for the silver lining in your own reality. It forces us to find hope where others might only experience angst. It's where we find evolving relationships, unexpected treasures, humor, humility, and blessings. Sometimes the gifts appear obvious and immediate. Other times we don't see the gifts for some time, and they are subtle.

So I guess a fair way to look at this philosophy would be to say that in every experience we have in life, there are gifts and there are struggles. Liam's time spent in Texas for eleven weeks straight is the perfect example of this idea. There were certainly many struggles! I was forced to constantly leave one child behind to be with the other. I worried myself sick that both of them would develop some kind of abandonment syndrome. Liam hated it when we'd leave him after each visit, and the look on his face often haunted me. If both of them needed me at a moment's notice, I simply could not be in two places at one time.

Now let's look at the gifts. Some of them were immediately evident and helped me breathe. I loved the head nurse on his unit from the very beginning, and she encouraged me to call and check on him whenever I needed to. I could tell the other children on the unit were emotionally connected to the staff. Children are not good at hiding such emotions. Over time I realized many other gifts. For example, for the first time in as long as I could remember, I got to be just "Momma." I wasn't Liam's nurse, therapist, pharmacist, or restrainer. It brings tears to my eyes just thinking about how much I cherished this gift! I also got much needed one-on-one time with Mira, which was priceless. Mira got to explore who she was without the influence of having a special-needs brother around. Most importantly, all three of us learned we are stronger than we ever could have imagined.

I have learned to look for the gifts because otherwise I will spend all my energy focusing on the struggles. Yes, there *are* struggles! Some of them feel insurmountable. Yet with each and every situation, we take something away that is positive. So many of the days in the lives of special-needs families are exceedingly challenging, so I have also accepted that the gifts are often found in tiny, little packages.

Recently, Liam had a really low-functioning day. He was agitated, grumpy, sensory overloaded, and very snappy at Mira. I was exhausted and, quite frankly, couldn't wait for him to go to bed. We snuggle every night before he falls asleep, and that night, while we were lying there, he grabbed my arm and pulled it tightly around him. I knew he needed the sensory input to help him settle down. But the next thing he did was amazing. He kissed my hand and said, "Thank you for taking care of me, Mom."

This moment, this fraction of our very long day, was such a gift. He knew I would be there for him, took solace in my presence, and let me know how he was feeling. It wiped my slate clean and allowed me to lie there with my sweet angel, just breathing in the brief moment of peace. I knew this wasn't going to be our new status quo. Liam would likely wake up as agitated as he was the morning before. However, in the middle of all the chaos, I received a gift. It made that day somehow easier to put behind me. I fell asleep with love in my heart, rather than dread for the sun's awakening.

The life of a zebra is not an easy one. It requires us to be hyperdiligent, overachieving, patient, tenacious, and compassionate. Many days, we have very little support while struggling to do the next right thing for our entire family. Be that as it may, we have the opportunity every single day that we wake to recognize the precious gifts that are sprinkled along our path. Relish them, catalog them in your mind, and use them as momentum to propel you down the road less traveled.

Chapter 22

There Is Always Hope!

There have been days I simply believed there was absolutely nothing I could do about the reality of my life. Those have been my worst days. They were the kind of days where I wanted to curl up in a ball, under a blanket, in my closet, with the light off. Looking back on those days, one thing really seems to stand out. I had lost hope.

If you really think about it, there is *never* no hope. There is *always* something to hope for. Maybe at a given moment you are too exhausted, angry, sad, resentful, or hopeless to see this, but, regardless, it is true. If we have hope, we have yet another place to begin. I believe with hope, the possibilities are endless.

Inspiring hope was the number one reason I wrote this book. I hoped that my candid truth would, at the very least, give you hope. I wanted to share with you all the gifts I've found along the way and how those gifts have allowed me to continue to have hope. I hope that you have come to believe that hope comes in all shapes and sizes.

Through humility, humor, and friendship, we find hope. Behind the scary doors of the unknown, we encounter hope. After we have survived the unthinkable, there lies hope. Standing beside fellow zebras, we discover hope. Hope is yet another gift. It changes how we look at our reality. In a lot of ways, our hope for the future is more important than our present truth. The mind is an extraordinarily powerful force. It protects us even when we don't know how to protect ourselves. With hope, we are empowered to rewrite our own stories and to decide *this is not going to be how our stories end*!

Appendix A

The Power of Words

Quotes are everywhere in my home. They are written on plaques, framed, and even hung on my refrigerator. They inspire, motivate, and ground me. A single quote can become my mantra for the day, week, or even the year, helping me gain or change my perspective. Below you will find many of my favorite quotes. I hope they will be as helpful to you as they have been to me.

"God, grant me the serenity to accept the things I cannot change, the courage to change the things I can, and the wisdom to know the difference." ~Reinhold Niebuhr

"May your choices reflect your hopes, not your fears." ~Nelson Mandela

"Promise me you'll always remember: You're braver than you believe, stronger than you seem, and smarter than you think." ~A.A. Milne

"You never know how strong you are until being strong is the only choice you have." ~Bob Marley

"Insanity: doing the same thing over and over again and expecting different results." ~Albert Einstein

"Everybody is a genius. But if you judge a fish by its ability to climb a tree, it will live its whole life believing that it is stupid." ~Albert Einstein

"Anyone can give up...it's the easiest thing to do. But to hold strong when everyone else expects you to fall apart, now that's true strength." ~Chris Bradford

"Courage doesn't always roar. Sometimes courage is the little voice at the end of the day saying, 'I'll try again tomorrow.'" ~Mary Anne Radmacher

"Sometimes the things we can't change end up changing us." ~Author Unknown

"A friend is someone who knows the song in your heart and can sing it back to you when you have forgotten the words." ~Donna Roberts

"If you don't like where you are, move. You are not a tree." ~Author Unknown

"I've learned that people will forget what you said, people will forget what you did, but people will never forget how you made them feel." ~Maya Angelou

"God changes caterpillars into butterflies, sand into pearls, and coal into diamonds using time and pressure— He's working on you too." ~Rick Warren

"Holding on to anger is like drinking poison and expecting the other person to die." ~Gautama Buddha

"Isn't it funny how day by day nothing changes, but when you look back, everything is different..." ~C. S. Lewis

"Do the best you can until you know better. Then when you know better, do better." ~Maya Angelou

"I'm thankful for my struggle because without it I wouldn't have stumbled across my strength." ~Alex Elle

"Normal is an illusion. What is normal for the spider is chaos for the fly." ~Charles Addams

"Don't base your decisions on the advice of those who don't have to deal with the results." ~Author Unknown

"Hardships often prepare ordinary people for an extraordinary destiny." ~C. S. Lewis

"Wouldn't it be nice if the world was flat...? That way we could just push off the people we don't like!" ~Author Unknown

"Hope is being able to see that there is light despite all of the darkness." ~Desmond Tutu

"No one can make you feel inferior without your consent." ~Eleanor Roosevelt

"Most people are good, and some people suck." ~Kelly C. Miltimore

"At any given moment, you have the power to say, this is *not* how the story is going to end!" ~Author Unknown

Appendix B

Motivating Music

"Music is what feelings sound like."
~Author Unknown

Music often transports me to a place of new energy and possibilities. I have several songs that I listen to, in particular, when I need a boost or an internal pep talk. While Liam was hospitalized in Chicago a friend texted me a link to the song "Guardian," by Alanis Morissette. She told me it was my theme song and I have listened to it hundreds of times since that day. Frequently I listen to it while I'm running and I think to myself, if Liam can endure what he has, I can certainly make it another mile!

Below I am including the names of other songs that help me get out of a funk. I encourage you to create a list of motivators, whatever they may be, to help you stay the course when your service-engine light comes on.

Other Inspirational Songs

"Brave" by Sara Bareilles

"Don't Stop Believin'" by Journey

"Best Day of My Life" by American Authors

"If You're Going Through Hell" by Rodney Atkins

"You're Not Alone" by Marie Miller

"Unwritten" by Natasha Bedingfield

"You Get What You Give" by New Radicals

"Fighter" by Christina Aguilera

"Roar" by Katy Perry

"Little Miss" by Sugarland

"The Best" by Tina Turner

"Born This Way" by Lady Gaga

"The Climb" by Miley Cyrus

"Stronger" by Kelly Clarkson

"Secrets" by Mary Lambert

Made in the USA
San Bernardino, CA
25 January 2015